The Experience
A Celebration of Being

The Experience
A Celebration of Being

Sirio Esteve

Photographs by James L. McGuire

Random House
New York

To Eugenia

Library of Congress Cataloging in Publication Data

Esteve, Sirio.
The experience: A celebration of being

1. Meditations. I. Title.
BV4832.2.E8 1974 242 72-11425
ISBN 0-394-48322-7

Manufactured in the United States of America
Design by Bernard Klein
98765432

First Edition

Foreword

He said to the people, "Sing high. Do not stifle the song in your heart." And the people said, "We are hungry. We sing low and sad." He said to the people, "Stand and demand." And the people said, "We are sick and we are tired." He said to the people, "Know yourselves. There is glory in you." And the people said, "We know our burdens and frustrations, our problems and anxieties, our hardships and our suffering."

"Are those in power like you?" He asked. "Are they burdened and beaten?" And the people said, "They are not. They are rich. They are respected and honored." Then He said, "They have taken your share and theirs, and allowed you a pittance. That is not just. Claim your rights." And the people said, "When we claim our rights, they jail us; they defame us; they ostracize us." He bows His head and says nothing. The people bow their heads and say nothing. The planet turns slowly toward midnight and despair.

Now He speaks again. "Do not despair," He says. "Creativity is on our side. Love is on our side. Beauty is on our side. Truth is on our side. Miracles are on our side. We cannot lose. Look at the stars. They dispel the blackness of the night. They, too, are on our side. Stand up and celebrate." A fire runs through the people. They clench their fists and raise their arms. "We will fight," they say. "We will demand our rights," they say. "We will achieve justice," they say, "for ourselves and all men."

Sirio Esteve

Contents

The Man

He came and stayed awhile. At first He perplexed us. Who was He? Later we accepted Him as the man that is mankind.

No man can describe Him. When He has a face or body, it is the face or body of someone seen during the day—a woman walking leisurely, young, attractive, tall, the bag in her hand hanging low on a long strap, or a man speaking barbarous words while dark currents of sorrow swirl through him, drawing him into despair. He appears in anyone at all whom we encounter when our acceptance is open: in strangers who, though different in language and belief, are perceived as one of us on the way all men follow to wherever it is all men go.

We recognize Him the way we recognize our friends—by the special effect He has upon us. When He comes to our house, we change in the way which only He can incite. The contours of our sensibility and our thinking move out to embrace all existence. By this change we are magically united, without loss in individuality, to the city and the men who built, maintain and live in it.

When He first came to our house, He spoke little. Perhaps we lacked ears for Him. Perhaps the ground for speech had to be prepared. At that time our knowledge of Him consisted in an experience sufficiently recognizable on recurrence to warrant the words "Good day. Welcome back."

During His stay, sometimes a matter of minutes, all men were acceptable. That established His presence. It was not "yes" to one man, "no" to another, and "maybe" to the rest. It was "yes" to all without exception. Since total acceptance is not easily sustained, He would soon vanish. A response adverse to Him would arise and push Him out. When that happened, the aloneness we felt confirmed His departure.

Clouds curtain the sky. Fog conceals the sea. Our smallness asserts itself. He has gone away.

Where does He go when He leaves? None of us knows with certainty. Was He pushed into an inner darkness by our narrow and petty attachments, where He waits patiently for an occasion to return? One thing is certain, His separation from us does not separate Him from others. Across the street or on the other side of the globe is where He is after He has left us. Up on a mountain or down in a valley or on the land between, all at the same time; that is where He is. On the high seas or in the stratosphere going in opposite directions without pulling apart; wherever mankind separately receives Him; that is where He is, one experience in many places, busily building the House of Mankind.

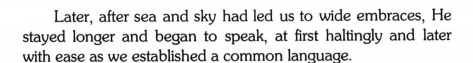

Later, after sea and sky had led us to wide embraces, He stayed longer and began to speak, at first haltingly and later with ease as we established a common language.

Come! Welcome Him into the house of our consciousness; know Him as a profound manifestation of yourself; sail or fly with Him into the realm of mankind; become a man among men where each man is a man among men without loss in identity.

The House of Mankind

❦

The gulls wheel and gather in forlorn groups. Their plaintive cries pierce the air. For whom do the gulls grieve? For whom? For themselves? For men? For unknown existence?

For whom do they cry in the sad cadences of gray and white, brown and blue?

Their cry evokes a yearning: clean, wild and unclaimed like the salt in far-reaching waters.

Rise, men, to the cry of gulls; rise to the salt, pure and wild as oceans. Rise and abolish the separations which contaminate men.

The House of Mankind is a divided house beset with discord.

Indeed, it is a house beset with discord everywhere on the six continents where its structure rises. What is this thing which separates men?

It is a boundary: a mark of possession indicating that the territory within belongs to some but not to others. Men live in compounds called nations. The House of Mankind is a divided house beset with national rivalries.

5

And what are these organizations which contend with one another: these alliances, associations, assemblies, clubs, unions, societies?

They are occupational and class distinctions which categorize men and grant them special privileges. By them one man can have what another man cannot have. The House of Mankind is a divided house beset by the assumption that position and status confer privileges on some to be denied to others.

And who are these cozy groups and those withdrawn individuals?

The first are kinfolk who place great importance on their issuance from the same womb and by the same organ of fertilization: the first family, the second family, the third family and the families of no consequence. The second are rugged individualists: men who stand apart and aloof with an allegiance limited to themselves and their peers. The kinfolk convert the House of Mankind into apartment complexes. The rugged individual-

ists convert it into private dwellings. The House of Mankind is a divided house beset with separations and discord, more makeshift than plan, more dream than reality. The House of Mankind is a house disrupted by the divisions in men.

Jetties. Dark! Wet! Out-reaching! Resisting the onrush, back-pull and side-sweeps of dynamic tides. Reverent before the glory of ocean and sky.

Behold the parable of jetties: of reverence, power and glory; firm as mountain rock, dynamic as sea water, open as sky space.

Behold and learn, so that the House of Mankind may be a house united by reverence for existence: reverence for existence before the power and glory of existence: reverence for existence before the power and glory slumbering in human existence. Behold, learn and strive.

There are people who sing for us; who laugh for us and dance for us. People who heal us; take our hands and lead us: people who love us.

Take our hands and tell us how to build our house.

Not by treaties!

No!	*Not by laws!*
No!	*Not by authority!*
No!	*Not by threats!*
No!	*Not by promises!*
No!	*Not by visions!*
No! Enough of "not by." By what, then? Tell us by what.	*By experience!*
Of what?	*By experience of Me. By the mankind in you which makes each man as important as others; not allowing appearance, condition, position, attainment to change it.*
	Are you human by birth? Then you are one of us.
He killed a man.	*That does not change it.*
He will kill other men.	*That does not change it. A man is the responsibility of all. Reach to him compassionately. Touch him kindly.*
He will kill me.	*Show your concern. Accept him as you accept a friend, and he will kill no one. Killing made a killer of him. Only kindness and acceptance will cure him.*
I will do it for myself and for mankind.	*The House of Mankind is built*

by an acceptance as free as the embracing openness of oceans. It is built by you yourself busy at the task of developing your humanity by the best sensitivity in you. It is built by men meeting men as equals. Seek the one in you that is all men without ceasing to be individual men and you will build the House of Mankind.

In experience lies the future: in expanding experience lies the future of mankind: in the amalgamations of experience lie the amalgamations of men which build the House of Mankind, now threatened by divisions; by the smallness in men overcoming the greatness in them to produce a divided house leaning toward destruction; by attempts to preserve and exalt the parts without regard for the whole structure. In mankind lies the salvation of men. There and no place else.

True, indeed. Say it again.

In mankind lies the salvation of men. There and no place else.

Thank You for Your words. We will convert them into experience. We will be You.

Slavery

When the idea of service first emerged in life, it said, "Surrounding conditions are the law. Obey them or die." Life obeyed and survived, for in obeying natural law it was served.

When men arrived, some men used the idea of service for personal gain. They said, "Obey and serve us and we will pay you. Your survival depends upon it." Men obeyed and many died because the service was difficult and the payment inadequate.

THAT IS HOW THE IDEA OF SERVICE
DEGENERATED INTO THE IDEA OF SLAVERY.

Are You beholden to anyone? *Of course.*

To whom? *To men.*

In what way? *In the way of service.*

By compulsion? *No.*

How, then? *In accordance with human needs.*

To what end? *The House of Mankind.*

Can You be converted into actions which destroy mankind? *No.*

How do You escape it?

I am the experience that amalgamates men. When action becomes destructive, I am annulled.

Ego produced a slave society. By ego, men brutalize all things near them. Nothing touched by it escapes defilement except by withdrawal.

Ego is a natural deficiency of immaturity that brutalizes ideas.

End the debasement of mankind by ego. Cleanse your ideas and yourselves by ending the slavery ego has instituted.

Slavery as men practice it is the most obscene idea of all. By placing men in classes and compelling lowly placed men to obey highly placed men, it sanctions the distinctions "Superior" and "Inferior" and fosters the antagonisms natural to it. No society stressing and exploiting class distinctions can bring the House of Mankind to completion.

Service as a universal feature appears in the interrelated dependence of existences. The various units of existence serve each other in ways which maintain the whole. In this sense, the planets are restricted by their universal interrelation. Life is restricted by its earthly environment. Selfhood is restricted by its bodily location.

These positional restrictions pertain to the universal structure. They maintain the structure and its characteristics. The tendency is constructive. It is not a case of one existence enforcing its will upon another. It is a case of all existences working together to form a universe. Ideas here function as they

should function. In men, ideas may become agents of personal ambition. They may function to retard human development by building societies on slave foundations.

Come and do my bidding.
Yes, sir.
You have the instructions. Follow them.
Yes, sir.
Attention!
Yes, sir.
March!
Yes, sir.
Shoot!
Yes, sir.

What is this game called?   *The brutalization of mankind.*

How is it achieved?   *By the whip:*
The leather whip,
The economic whip,
The social whip,
The legal whip,
The contract whip,
The military whip,
The power whip,
The addiction whip.
By the whip, with the help of
the squeeze.

What squeeze?   *The money squeeze.*

Tell us about the money squeeze.   *To do that, I must tell you about the belly and the ego.*

The human animal has two prominent features: one purely physical, called The Belly, and one mostly human, called The Ego. The belly is a sack which must be filled daily in order to keep its owner alive. The substance placed in the sack is called food. Some of it comes free; most of it must be bought. This produces the money squeeze. The belly says, "Get money, no matter how, to keep us alive." So the owner of the belly submits to abuse when necessary, in order to keep his belly and himself alive. This places him at the beck and call of those who offer money for services, and it allows those who offer the money to convert service into slavery. The slavery, however, must be disguised. Modern emancipation permits no slavery other than disguised slavery.

Ego, the second source of the money squeeze, works more subtly than its compatriot, the Belly. It thrives on possessions. A man must have a place in the world. How is he to have a place in the world if he does not own valuable things, such as a car, a home, a color television? These possessions demonstrate that he amounts to something. He must prove this to other men to gain their admiration and retain his own self-respect. So he hires himself out to earn the money with which to buy his possessions.

Of course he is a free man. He does not have to work for anyone whom he does not choose to serve. However, if he does not work, money will not be forthcoming. Consequently he works for those who pay him best even when they pay little. The money squeeze has placed hands on him. The tightness of the hold is determined by circumstances. Does the victim have dependents? How old is he? Has he been successful? What economic situation prevails at the time? Who rules the nation? These and other factors will determine the extent of the pressure; and the extent of the pressure will establish the degree of slavery.

Contemporary slavery works like a slot machine. A man gives his service; out comes ninety-eight cents minus tax. Perhaps he can live on it. Perhaps he cannot. That's his problem.

The externals of slavery have changed. Such crudities as chains and balls have been abandoned. Nowadays, slaves and nonslaves dress alike except in the armed forces. There the degree of slavery is indicated by a uniform. Employees in commerce and industry hardly realize the ignominy to which they have fallen. They go back to the grind day after day, glad to have a job or position which meets or partially meets the needs of their bellies and their egos. That is slavery in the factory, the office, the assembly line, the transportation system, in all activity related to business.

In early slavery, a man worked for the benefit of his master. For this he received food, clothing, housing and some leisure. The binding factor was obedience and work for the master who captured or bought him.

In modern slavery, a man works for the benefit of his employer. For this he receives the means with which to procure food, clothing, housing and some leisure. The binding factor is to obey and work for his employer. Indeed, a modern slave can change his employer at will. He also receives better food, clothing, housing and leisure. Nevertheless, the relation is basically the same. A man obeys and works for another man instead of working for himself or society. To work under orders in an enterprise in which the material gain goes mostly to another places a man in a slave position.

The change which has occurred in the slave-master relation blinds most men to the remaining similarities. Men born into a society having slavery as an established feature fail to perceive the actual situation, especially when care is taken to conceal it. An industrial society must have buyers to remain solvent. Therefore, salaries must be sufficiently high to permit the buying of houses, cars, televisions and other good things. People having the means for these purchases will say, "We are free. We do as we like with our money. If we don't like our employer, we can seek another."

This affirmation reveals the type of inculcation foisted on our youth. The prevalent concept of freedom favors egotism. Men are free to rise above other men and exploit them. They are free to build empires of their own. They are free to perpetuate social structures which place masses of people in disadvantageous positions. Here freedom is a prize to be won through inheritance, competitive confrontations and egotistic dedications. In this relationship, freedom, justice and equal opportunity for all are promises running counter to the mainstream of events.

While this type of freedom remains, many will be pushed into slave positions because slavery has been institutionalized and sanctioned. There is no future for mankind in that.

Listen.   *I'm here.*

Can a man be a slave if he eats
well?   *Yes.*

And dresses well?   *Yes.*

If he has money to spend as he likes to spend it?   *Yes.*

Is slavery a benign institution, the best possible at present?   *No.*

Do You participate in it?   *No.*

How do You avoid it?   *By accepting and treating all men as equals.*

Is slavery a vicious institution?   *It is abusive, insensitive, divisive, humiliating, thwarting.*

Can a man escape from it?   *Yes.*

How?   *By accepting and treating all men as equals.*

You point to a new world?   *I do.*

To one in which service is not brutalized?   *I do.*

We will try to follow You to it.

Death

By the way of service, mankind comes to life.
By the way of slavery, it moves toward death.

Is it to be more life or less life? Is it to be service or slavery?

They sit around at the funeral home; whispering, reminiscing, telling about this person or that person, laughing when words or a situation amuses them, offering gratuitous advice with references to health and success; and, of course, with allusions to that most important of importances, the king pin and queen lady of organized amusement, the real experience among experience — the act by which a man and woman are genitally joined to each other.

You tickle me and I will tickle you; in that way we will forget about slavery and death.

Skip us. We are busy doing nothing.
We can be pleasant, polite, concerned in small ways. We are architects of the surface. We know how to polish it. We glamorize it. When we are together, life has a nice appearance. Like morticians, we inject charm into death.

Who would deny these people their death? They prefer to live in a room; let them live in a room. They prefer to talk about themselves; let them talk about themselves. Indeed, their eyes open wide when they see a man on the moon. After expressions of amazement and approval, their lids contract to the compass of the neighborhood and some "good" friends. May peace be with them all their dying days!

Men and women, who know how, give birth to themselves many times over as the day proceeds. Should they fail in this, the day loses its luster. More existence, primarily for the whole of it, but also for instances of it, is the function of birth. By birth existence knows itself better. Since death is not to know, birth annihilates death as it preserves the universe. It is the resurrection, the savior, the hope, the fulfillment. Only it can save a moribund mankind.

Birth requires movement. No one achieves it by a standstill. Are you going somewhere? If so, you may have a child; not necessarily one of humanly fashioned flesh after a nine-month interim, but one in which gleams of new existence brighten your mind. In the latter case, you have given birth to yourselves; and you may do it again and again without a nine-month wait.

This is not accomplishable, however, at coffee klatsches, cocktail parties or family gatherings where everyone talks excitedly about what has been. The past cannot conceive a child. What-is must be around to manage it. Even then the attempt will fail unless what-will-be lends assistance.

If you attain birth often, you need not worry about the future. You belong to it and you will learn more about existence as you live. If you are too tired to achieve birth in yourself, you can still retain a hold on the future by parenthood.

Parenthood is a way of service. Perhaps the most rewarding way.

We have children to raise. Do not speak to us of death.

Come, child. Let me help you. Let me guide you. Let me find my future in yours.

We made a child out of us. Then another and another. Do not speak to us about living death.

By our children we pertain to the resurrection. They came out of us when we joined our bodies. Now we come out of them each day as we serve them.

Let it be so. Let men be saved by their children. When their children leave, give them the strength to be saved out of themselves.

To fall back now to the narrow circles of memory, gossip, regrets, complaints; to dwell on the fact that they are gone, sooner than might have been or in ways not agreeable, is to slip back toward death and bring mankind back with oneself.

There they sit, the ungrateful ones, unfaithful to the light of their childhood and their children's childhood. Sterile. Universal misanthropes. Weights on the future.

Mankind trudges along in darkness century after century on all continents with constant depletions and renewals, like an army in the field being subdued by death as it seeks to annihilate death.

Is there a hidden enemy in the enemy?	*There is.*
Who is it?	*Slavery.*
You mean that slavery leads to death?	*I do.*

We had a good time and forgot about our slavery. Now we are ready to return to it.

Slavery accounts for the reverses, the standstills and the slowdowns which affect individuals and societies. It is directly responsible for the moribundity found in the race.

To vitalize the race, abolish slavery. To do this, men must recognize slavery as slavery, despite the disguises it might wear. Men who are compelled by need and law to do what they do not wish to do are slaves to the extent to which they do it, and at the same time are candidates for moribund forms of leisure.

To avoid this, serve in ways which add to selfhood. Would you work tomorrow if you did not have to, because the work itself brings fulfillment? If so, you are free and not in need of moribund diversions. Service cures. It heals death. Even in age, remain attached to service. Otherwise your existence will dwindle and die, even as you live.

Service is light. Follow it.

The sea serves the sky. The sky serves the sea. Together they produce the miracle of sky and sea. Learn to serve others as you serve yourself. Then you and they will produce the miracle of mankind.

Deception

Do You lie?

No. I appear when men do not lie. I am an experience. Experiences do not lie. Men lie about them deliberately or out of ignorance. When I am in men, men are in each other. I am a living thing, not an arrangement of words. An arrangement of words falsely claiming to be Me cannot elicit the experience I am.

Agreed! Words lie. You are not words even when You incite words. However, eyes can lie, smiles and laughter can lie, gestures can lie. Nonetheless, agreed! You are not a glance, a smile or a gesture. As experience You are total.

I reach from continent to continent. I include isolated men living in jungle and polar regions. Where a man is, I am, mostly unseen and unreceived, because men shun the truth out of fear and ignorance.

25

Come sit cozily at my side and lie. In my turn, I will lie to you. In a lying world, to lie is right.

How will we understand ourselves if we don't understand our lying? Lies, some big, some small, keep the world ticking.

You come along. I come along. We meet. You tell the truth and some lies. I tell the truth and some lies. We part. You go your way. I go my way.

Tell us, sir, why do we lie?

Sometimes for the fun of it, but mostly to retain respect for ourselves. Sometimes to hurt people. Always we lie to gain a wanted thing we would lose if we spoke truthfully.

Let you put me down? I will not permit it. So I lie. Lose my possessions, my privileges, my superiority? Unthinkable!

I value the lie. It fires my flesh, incites my lust. By it, living things come to be good things, heartwarming things which banish the distress of truth.

Evidently you speak of an ocean of lies in which men bathe daily.

And also of a sky of truth where men dream nightly. Unless alloyed with truth, lies will not hold together.

In a civilization some men want to be smarter than others in everything, or at least in some specialty. When two such meet, tremors shake the foundations of their houses. To be smarter than all one's acquaintances put together, one must be a clever liar. So it comes to be that on earth, smart liars lead the truthful into make-believe.

"It cannot be different," says an apologist blandly. Speak to him about poverty. "It cannot be different," he says, "some must remain hungry." Speak to him about disease and injustice. "It cannot be different," he says, "it pertains to human nature." Speak to him about war. "It cannot be different," he says, "the Bible predicts it."

Come again to dreams; once more endlessly. The true dream relies upon experience and builds by it. It is not a lie even when men lie about it. It is existence speaking about wonders to come. Believe in it. Work for it. It will not forsake you.

Existence has places to go beyond the place where it is. You have places to go beyond the place where you are. Oppose the nonexistence of your culture. Expose it. Expose the lies, the make-believe, the idolatry, the buffoonery. Do it in a simple way. Do not conform. Escape the noose by walking right on past the lies. Mankind depends upon you! Right on past the lies. The police will gang up on you. The army will be called into action. The courts will see that you receive "just" punishment. But they will not destroy you. The forces of existence uphold you. What must be will be. The House of Mankind will rise toward completion and drive all lies out of human existence.

Simplicity

The first of two men who were discussing simplicity said, "I am the most simple of all men." The second replied, "It cannot be. No one is more simple than I." "I am more simple," said the first. "On what do you base your contention?" asked the second. "Because I never lie except out of ignorance," replied the first. "In that case I am simpler than you," insisted the second. "Why?" asked the first. "Because I, too, never lie except out of ignorance. But I am less ignorant than you; therefore, more simple," replied the second.

A simple man walks straight, talks straight, thinks straight and acts straight. His complex brothers walk roundabout, talk roundabout, think roundabout and act roundabout. They do not enter into the core of existence.

Jump in.

Into what?

Into existence.

I am in.

In an outside way.

I don't understand.

By words, gestures, memories, anticipations, ties, subterfuges, histrionics, routine, directives, compulsions — indirectly and complicatedly. Take off your clothes and jump in.

You mean naked?

With your skin close to exist-ence, eyes and ears vibrant with images and sounds, mind bright with light—in a direct and simple way. Immerse yourself. Men do not advance from simplicity to complexity. Nothing is more complicated than ignorance and dissem-blance.

Explain Yourself. Your simplic-ity is not easily understood.

It was said, "Life is simple and it became complex." And it is true. Then it was said, "Men are simple and they become complex." But it is wrong, because knowing begins in the complexity of bewilderment and advances to the simplicity of comprehension.

Shall I bring in Omniscience to clarify the matter?

If anything can clarify it, Om-niscience should be able to. We did not know that You are an associate of Omniscience.

Mankind is, in a way, but I meant something else. I meant the idea of Omniscience. An intelligence equal to the uni-verse does not find the uni-verse complicated. In its per-

ception, the universe is beautifully simple; lucid everywhere in the light of understanding.

The idea thrills us. What a dream is Omniscience! We understand that nothing is complicated for Omniscience. What relevance does that have to our problem?

It indicates that existence is more or less inclusive; not more or less complicated. To men it seems complicated when they lack the power to perceive it clearly. The complexity is a subjective state produced by ignorance. The universe is as complicated as men are ignorant.

We understand what You mean, but in being subject to the hallucinations of men, we are not certain about the truth of it. You say that to have ten or twelve features instead of two or three does not complicate existence. It is to have more features, not more complexity. Complexity occurs when a perceiver unable to understand aspects of existence connects them in wrong ways or introduces extraneity into them. As You see it, existence itself is simple; so simple that complex men cannot understand it.

That is my assertion. Nothing existential is intrinsically complicated. Only human ideas about it are complicated. Nothing in total existence needs an explanation. Men need explanations because they perceive and experience less than the whole. This leads to false explanations and a false complexity. A simple man stays within the fluid bounds of experience as he tries to understand existence. He acknowledges the limits of his knowledge and does not conclude that existence is complex because it seems so. To him the universe is mysterious rather than complex.

We grant it. Existence is simple when the intellect is equal to it, and complicated when the intellect is not; therefore, nothing is more complicated than ignorance.

❀

Simple folk are those who have accepted truth as a way of life and have thus avoided the complications of false living. Evidently their life-enmeshed intelligence will not sail spaceships to other planets, nor will it win Asiatic or other wars. This excludes simple folk from participation in the two most complicated undertakings of our times. Moreover, their intelligence will not be able to organize great commercial enterprises, establish powerful, political systems, invent erudite cosmic explanations, enforce subtle or crass class distinctions, manage luxurious recreational facilities. It provides poorly for the things complex men want most. Their intelligence, nevertheless, is placed highest by Him because its trueness helps to build the House of Mankind.

Step forward and we will decide whether or not we are truly simple.

When a man knows himself, he can be true to himself and the existence around him. When he knows a little about himself, he can be true to the little he knows. When he knows almost nothing about himself, his trueness to himself and the existence around him amounts to almost nothing.

Do we know ourselves?   *Somewhat.*

What do we know?   *Mostly we know how we act and why.*

Does that produce knowledge of self?

It can. As we observe the methods we use to attain our goals and how and why we deviate from our course, we learn about ourselves. We learn also whether we follow The Way of Deception or The Way of Truth or how we fluctuate between the two.

It follows then that we can be true to ourselves to a degree.

It does.

When we do it, we are simple.

To the degree to which we do it.

When we are true to the self, the self evolves. As it evolves, it reaches more existence. As it reaches more existence, it breaks away from superficial attachments. As it breaks away from superficial attachments, it helps to build the House of Mankind. Thus it is that simple people build the House of Mankind.

How superficial are we?

As superficial as we are complicated.

When is living complicated?

When it abandons the main currents of existence and loses itself in details.

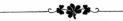

Are details not related to existence?

They are, in a way.

Why do You object to them?

Because they create off-center attitudes and lead men into labyrinths of nonsense.

One detail begets another detail. That detail begets another and another and another, forever if we wish, producing a magnificent edifice of details when we are clever. Now we have an elaborate way of life, only loosely connected with vital existence. Then we are complicated, not simple, and proud of it.

How do we avoid this?

Remain true to the sources of existence. New existence flows up in us each day; and it flows up in the existence accompanying ours.

How can we make the most of new existence?

By renouncing the periphery for the center. By saying "Now" instead of "Tomorrow" to the surge of selfhood. By courage and persistence. By loyalty to mankind. Mankind is the sun of our existence.

Existence thrives on existence. When incomplete, it advances by means of itself to more inclusive instances of itself. Men who resist this movement lose their hold on existence as it is in them and outside of them. Now they dedicate themselves to amusements, to superficialities, to detailed analyses and to other pastimes and endeavors which contribute little to existence's evolutionary surges. The House of Mankind cannot rely upon them for support. They are too complicated and important to be of service to it.

His existence watches existence pass by and he is sad. He tarries at the wayside, laughing and celebrating as existence passes by. And then he cries because it has passed by. He works strenuously, accumulates money and becomes famous as existence passes by; but he is not happy with his money and his success. He has not been true to his existence. He has let it pass by.

As existence passes by, he lies to it and to himself to compensate for the loss of existence caused by its passing by. As he lies, he moves further and further away from existence and loses sight of it. Now he says that existence stands still, but he is deceived. His lying has deceived him. "All for nothing," he says, as death approaches. Again he is wrong. Existence has more time than he has.

Elaborate artificiality cannot remain. Deliberate deception cannot remain. Barbarous destruction cannot remain. Existence will not permit it. It directs men to simple solutions. It speaks through itself. When human, it praises or condemns itself.

Believe in mankind's emancipation or not, as you prefer, and speak in accordance with your preference. When you say "No," your existence speaks against the existence of those who say "Yes." Existence against existence? It cannot last. The "No" and "Yes" must combine to produce a more complete existence. That is our faith.

In years ahead, men will achieve the full meaning of their humanity. Existence did not become human to lessen the achievements of animals. This animal, the final one, carries the banner of consciousness to higher significances. What at present are dreams will govern the activities of future cultures. In achieving the advance, the human animal will move away from his animal nature to solidify the nature of consciousness. This heralds the annihilation of the animal as the awareness of self and universe evolves.

Do we love the animal in us?	*We do.*
To what extent?	*As much as it assists the development of selfhood.*
Do we love it when it impedes selfhood?	*We do not.*
We object then to the reduction of the animal into an instrument of pleasure by abuses of sensory and generative organs?	*We do.*

And also to the self-indulgence of excessive ornamentation?	*We do.*
And also to the amassing of inordinate possessions?	*We do.*
And also to displays of personal importance?	*We do.*
We are simple folk.	*So be it.*
Attached to simple experiences.	*So be it.*
Lovers of existence.	*So be it.*
Devoted to its significances.	*So be it.*

When mankind achieves its fullness in a coming age, it will have been because of simple folk. They will have guided selfhood to fruition. The game is on now. Why don't we join it? The development has reached to here from a distant past and moves on to a more or less distant future. This century marks a position in the advance; perhaps a half or three quarters point. Who knows with certainty? That we are here and in it is certain.

As we look about we see others who are here with us. We read newspapers, listen to radio, look at television and learn about human action everywhere on the planet. And we are dismayed and discouraged by the brutality, the divisions and the hatred found in contemporary societies. Men have abandoned the simple ways of truth to follow violence into the complicated ways of wealth-sustained power. From the point of now, the House of Mankind seems never. However, present conditions do not end our hope.

Powerful, creative forces are at work in men and around

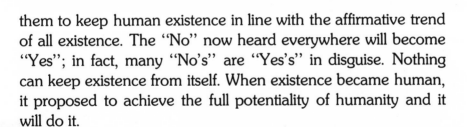

them to keep human existence in line with the affirmative trend of all existence. The "No" now heard everywhere will become "Yes"; in fact, many "No's" are "Yes's" in disguise. Nothing can keep existence from itself. When existence became human, it proposed to achieve the full potentiality of humanity and it will do it.

Ego

And we said to Him, have You

     No! No!

Who, then?   *Men!*

  The cry rose high over the din of the woods: "Me! Me! Me!" Men were loose on earth. That was long ago; long, long ago. So they say who know by hearsay.

  Indeed, a meticulous study was made. The compilation of evidence almost reaches the sky. Nevertheless, we know by hearsay, or book-say, or professor-say. What a day! What a day!

  Men were loose on earth. The cry "Me! Me! Me!," in whichever language said, inaugurated the beginning of mankind. Ah, me! Ah, me! And still, He says "Me, no."

How is that? If You are man-kind, how come no ego in You?

  "Me" is not mankind. "Us" is mankind. When Me beheld many not-Me's, the outgoing attachment Us began its earth-ly career. At that moment I appeared; that is, mankind

41

appeared and the building of mankind became first the covert and later the avowed purpose of human experience.

Us? Did You say "Us"?

We, not one or two; many.

Does 1 know 2? Does 2 know 3? One hundred numbers are here; do they know each other? A million numbers! Do they know each other?

How can they? Numbers are not self-aware. Only men know about each other in a clear way. Their self-awareness distinguishes between one man, ten men, one hundred men, one thousand men, one million men. What is more, they can be consciously interested and attached to each other; theoretically, up to three billion or more, the number of human beings living on earth at present. That is Us in the fullest sense.

Think about it. Three billion like yourself on earth now. Start where you are and go imaginatively to the people in the next town or city and then to the people in the next one, until you have reached all the towns and cities on earth; three billion, speaking different languages, following different customs and adhering to different faiths. Three billion; that is, Us in flux, because we move and because some are born and some die. Three billion: that is the size of our family at present. Can you feel attached to all of them; vaguely, of course, to those whom you have not and will not meet? If you can, He will draw you away from the narrow ways of ego.

An egotist burrows a way through his own body. That is a narrow path to follow. Mercy!

An egotist sings a song to his own throat. That is a cheap music to live by. Mercy!

An egotist thinks in a frying pan by candlelight. That is a dark light by which to learn about a world. Sky and sun are needed for that; but an egotist uses a frying pan and a candle. Mercy! Mercy! Mercy!

For whom?

For all who feel and act and think from within the compounds of their skin.

How else, you ask?

Evidently a biologist questions our assertion. Indeed, the self looks at its body from eyes in it. It feels the body by nerves in it. It thinks about the body by a brain in it. Simultaneously, it looks at the world, feels it and thinks about it in the same way—from within the compounds of the skin. A man who conceives himself in this fashion has taken a good position from which to understand himself. But he disregards something of importance.

What does he disregard?

He disregards the immediate quality of his experience and the truth it reveals. In experience the self does not perceive itself as a brain looking out of eye windows, feeling by nerve antennae or thinking by word arrangements. When the self turns its attention on itself, it finds consciousness and identity reacting to the world from the features and qualities which it is. Selfhood has become sufficiently dominant to stand out as a distinct, conscious unit. The question to ask now is: "How engrossed is the self in its own importance?" It was natural in the beginning that a self-aware animal would become at least somewhat obsessed with itself as an individual. What happened as time passed? The obsession should have eventually lessened. Interest should have moved from the body, from possessions, from personal status; past the skin, over to other men and far places; and simultaneously inward into an enlarged selfhood, able to embrace mankind, the world and stars.

What, specifically, are the narrow ways of ego? In good living, Take and Give go together. Men give to others and they receive from others; and they enjoy both. This establishes a relation of mutual dependence and regard. This relation weakens and breaks when men imagine that they do not need others as much as others need them; or that mutual regard among a limited few suffices. Now, Take gains a dominance over Give which may reach the extreme of taking as much as custom and law permit, and giving niggardly except where it enhances the position of the giver.

This attitude defines an egotist. An extreme egotist is a human animal who seeks in all feasible ways to enhance his own position with little or no regard for the detrimental effects his act has on others. In the egotist, one world becomes a reality or a near reality; one world as small, inhumane and stupid as a few individuals. This world of the egotist must not be confused with the one world sought by Him in which the regard of all men for each other creates a bond of oneness.

Take, in front, and Give, back there someplace, in service to Take, produce the narrow ways of the ego. When an instance of existence draws back from surrounding existence, it narrows its scope to little more than nothing. That, Mr. Egotist, is you; little more than nothing, regardless of how loud the band plays your tune. No one is important by himself. He needs to mingle freely with other existences to gain importance.

But how is he to mingle freely with other existences when he must preserve a grand image of himself as king, near-king, or should-be-king?

The following offenses are charged against egotists: First, egotists lose the full significance of social problems by concentrating on their personal implications. When the full significances are lost, minor significances usurp their place. Superficial, inhumane attitudes result from this. Second, egotists have lopsided intelligences, which lean toward them at the expense of truth. Self-deception and misrepresentation cannot be avoided here. Thus a world already false through ignorance becomes falser by the distortions of vanity. Third, egotists are oversensitive to damage done to them and insufficiently sensitive to damage done to others. Justice cannot function while this attitude prevails. Because of this, human relations become unjust personally, socially, nationally and internationally. In short, the self-love of the egotist fills the world with discord and hatred.

An egotist, no matter how grandly proportioned in his own eyes, has to admit that the sun is larger and brighter than he. If after making this sobering admission he can at times feel smaller than the sun, there is hope. He will not have to pass the rest of his life falling into booby traps set by his vanity.

The booby traps prepared by ego ensnare their victim with high promises. Unfortunately, after initial bounces the egotist finds himself at rest in low significance. His worldly rise was accompanied by an existential decline. A man has some sixty years to live. Not long, when one notices the quick demise of a year. Should the span contain seventy or eighty years, it is still a short time. Less than a century to parade about in immeasurable time.

With this in mind, the self may seek to aggrandize itself as an individual while it can. That only makes life shorter. Egotistic demands reduce the area of mingling. Self and world become less, and the time span is reduced by being limited to a content which pleases the ego.

Do you want a short life? Obey your ego. The booby traps it sets will guarantee a short life, regardless of the years you live.

An egotist needs a cleanser to clear away the corrosion consequent to narrow sentiment, abetted by narrow thinking leading to narrow values. He cannot, unfortunately, procure the cleanser at the supermarket, regardless of how super it may be. However, there is help for him if he has conceded that the sun is somewhat larger than he. Let him petition the sun. He can do this by singing Hallelujah to it. He will then be singing to something big instead of something small, something outside of him instead of something in him, something lasting instead of something temporal.

After he has earnestly placed the sun above him in its rightful position, he will be able to sing Hallelujah to smaller existences; and it may be that eventually he will sing Hallelujah to blades of grass or crests of waves. From there to the acceptance of most, and later to the acceptance of all men, is two small steps. Men, after all, are one in being men; fortunate or unfortunate, accomplished or unskilled, wise or ignorant, in health or in sickness, kind or cruel, egotistic or humble; one family sharing the exhilaration and distress of human existence.

Are you ample in affection and compassion? Do you think and act so as to assist the advancement of people? Do you celebrate achievements which free the people from the oppression of exploiters? Are your heart and mind with mankind in its struggle to rise out of ignorance and the failings of incompleteness? If you do not excel in these, you are undeveloped where development is most needed. If you have these attainments, you will not place yourself high above others, an untouchable in reverse; your action will not be controlled by notions of great superiority and importance; great masses of people will not seem to be intolerable and unworthy of esteem.

The sea engages our imagination. The sky challenges it.

The standing animal surveys his kingdom. "The earth," he says, "is ours. We, the species of man, are the first animals able to think and say that. No animal will rise above us in time ahead as we rose above our predecessors in life, for in us the animal denies himself."

Enough of animal. Something more, now. No higher animal will emerge out of men. It will be something different or nothing. The outcome depends upon us.

They amble along and forget. They worry and talk and forget. They speak beautifully about grand spectacles and they forget.

What is it they forget?

They forget that they are the last animal and the first instance of conscious existence. Intestines, a blood pump, air sponges, nerve slime and brain pulp have summoned a ghost; more exactly, three billion ghosts, making the earth the ghost planet.

Instances of existence had to announce themselves to other instances of existence. They had to shout "I am."

Existence not imbued with "I am" or an equivalent to it? Stay with the idea for a while. Billions of suns and planets; on earth, billions of simple and complex organisms and not a single "I am" in the whole of it? The idea will not stay with you. It can't. Your presence refutes it. When "I am" sounded in the earth's air, it proclaimed a new world for animals which would be superseded gradually by nonanimal worlds of consciousness.

Now the animal world weakens all around and in us, as ghostly selves seek to find a meaning in existence for ghostly selves. The dying is sad despite laughter, pomp, ornamentation, civility and make-believe. An end is the saddest occurrence, unbearably sad when the end does not release a beginning. Thus it is that the end of animals and plants and all the beauty they embodied had to and did inaugurate the beginning of identity and selfhood.

Salute all animals and plants near you. They achieved your birth. Soon they will decline. Their drama comes to an end as ours continues. Raise memorials to them in your sensitivity. Remain true to them and to yourself as one of them, even as you leave their world to enter into the self-worlds of consciousness.

Some rise on extended wings and circle in the air. Others remain quiet and impassive in the sun on the shore. Many centuries taught them their patience. The rumble of waves, the sweep of winds, daybreaks and nightfalls, seasons, tides, fog, rain pertain to them as their plumage does. The world outside blends intimately with the world inside.

When gulls and their brethren in life became men, the balance tipped. Inside assumed an importance it did not have. The magnification of "Me" came naturally as a consequence of consciousness located in an organism. The weak flicker of identity had to concentrate on itself in order to preserve itself. It thus converted "Mine" into the most meaningful aspect of existence; my body, my world, my children, my money, my position, my success, my sickness, my suffering, my mistakes, my misfortune. These "my's" weakened the relation of inner existence to outer existence. They created separate inner worlds not much interested in the great outside.

Men presently bogged down in the egotistic pleasures have a way out. They can perceive the way and follow it when their perception is clear. Nonhuman animals lack this perceptory assistance because they lack the consciousness required for it. Men know! Not inwardly and without awareness of it! They know sufficiently well to talk about their knowledge and act on it. They say "Do this," "Don't do that,"and they learn to do as they say.

That makes an oceanic difference. Men may not be able always to follow the directive. A well-prepared dinner can mean more than an eternity of stars when the dinner is on the table and the stars are in the sky. Nevertheless, a course can be charted and returned to when custom, momentary satisfactions and personal gain block the way out.

❈

Tell us about the course that annuls ego when the egotists are dissatisfied with their type of experience.

The egotist now seeks to love more extensively. Love for self expands into love for existence. When a man loves existence as existence, he loves men as men and he has ceased to be an egotist.

Men can enjoy the sky because it is a sky; the ground because it is ground; mankind because it is mankind; ideas because they are ideas; love because it is love; sharing because it is sharing. That is the new experience which redeems the egotist.

A pendulum swings to one side before swinging to the other. After that it swings in both directions. The self goes in, so that it may know and enjoy its small personal world. After that it goes out, so that it may know and enjoy mankind and the universe. When it succeeds in this, inner and outer existence blend as they do in gulls on the shore, but with a knowledge they lack.

An acorn takes moisture and light and sends a sprout through the earth up into the sky.

Why does it do it?

So that it may say "I am a beautiful oak"? It cannot be for that. The acorn does not know about itself. It does it in acorn fashion, for the sake of existence. It proclaims the motto "Unfoldment for the sake of unfoldment."

The seed of a man evolves in a womb. In time, it is pushed into an environment, later to be known as the earth. There it continues its development and learns about itself and the place of its existence.

What for? So that a man may strut about like a monarch, or long to do it when circumstance prevents it?

Not at all. Existence did not reveal a universe to men for them to ignore it. The inheritance makes demands. Existence revealed a universe to men for them to claim it. "How wonderful I am," though permissible as an episode, must change into "How wonderful the universe is." The ultimate enjoyment of men cannot be less than mankind and the portion of the universe open to mankind. When personal existence enjoys existence impersonally, it does not say "My sky." It says "Sky." It does not say "My friends." It says "Fellow-men." It does not say "My words." It says "Our conversation."

The prophetic sky waits. The oceanic cradle waits. Existence waits for itself everywhere, as it surveys itself. Men wait and strive, as time pushes them on to themselves. The beginning has been made. The advance continues. The culmination comes. The House of Mankind rises on itself to assume its sky-place.

Language

To speak to someone, anyone; to look from eyes to eyes comprehensively; to nod in agreement; to draw back in amazement; to be knowingly affected: everyday exchanges on the street, at the corner store, by telephone, in earnest or casually; a direct interaction between person and person, that in itself makes human experience cherishable.

To be out looking around is good. To find someone to greet is good. To mingle and share with another is good, and more so when the participants know about it. The experience of being a man among men is good. "Let it be again and again," say the participants, "for it is good."

Men have the privilege of language. In forest stillness they can speak. On the sea's desolation they can speak. While moonbound through soundless space they can speak.

By language we express our wishes. By it we advise each other. It allows a communication not possible for animals. Thinking, art, science, all inventions rely on it. When placed to good use, it stimulates progress. Have you put it to good use; have you learned by it, taught by it, rejoiced by it, consoled by it, guided by it, received by it, bestowed by it, assisted by it, amused by it, explained by it, loved by it, created by it? If you have, you will not be a complainer who speaks derogatorily about the earth and those who live on it.

Talk to someone. Listen to everything. Your alienation will vanish. You will be in. Men did not learn to speak in order to make noises.

Think well of men. They have performed marvelous feats. The invention of language is one of them.

A walking animal drew close to another. Both wore clothes. "What is it you want?" asked one animal. "To be near you," said the other. The animals clasped hands and walked away, talking all the time.

They talked and they understood each other. Whales, bears and condors would not have believed it possible had the idea entered miraculously into their minds. It took men to imagine and accomplish the miracle of verbal communication.

An animal did it. He built a skyscraper. What else? Airports and spaceships. What else? Music, like a symphony. What else? Hospitals, schools and libraries. What else? Look around. He built everything you see in the city and more. A great builder, this animal!

How did the animal do it? By verbal imagination!

Do nonspeaking animals have imagination? No. How can you tell? They build the same nest or dam, follow the same customs or rituals century after century. Before men came, a new behavior required a new form of life. Men broke this rigidity by the use of verbal imagination. It was a great feat. They deserve credit for it!

How did men acquire verbal imagination? Did they pick it up along the coast? Did it come down to them like light from the sky? Was it in the air to breathe? They must have found it somewhere.

Indeed, they found it somewhere; but not on the coast, or in the sky, or in the air. They found it under their skin.

Verbal imagination is a looking about in the mind by the mind itself for a way to solidify unformulated experience. The mind says, "How do I say it? How do I do it?" Then it makes up a statement or an explanation out of words, images, bits of knowing. It makes up something to show how it feels about an experience it has. It asserts; it proclaims; it promises. A mind-world replaces the flesh-world. Knowing triumphs over animality. It breaks habit and custom. Praise verbal imagination! It is the future!

I led a prosaic life because I was burdened. When I shed my burdens, I found imagination. It then propelled me toward the full meaning of selfhood.

Not even imagination can tell how imagination came to be. A birthday present, to be sure! From whom? Who can tell?

Do you think that He could tell us about its origin? He cannot tell us what we cannot imagine.

When a beaver meets a beaver, or an eagle an eagle, or a horse a horse, one does not say to the other, "Explain it to me." They cannot do that. They do not have a language or imagination of any consequence. Therefore animals, men excluded, do not have problems. They have difficulties which they solve existentially when they can.

Men have problems.

When an animal has language, imagination and a problem, he is human; and ideas come as naturally as fruit comes from flowers. An idea is a plan; an existential plan. It is also a solution; a way to proceed. It offers answers to why and wherefore. Ideas are the mainstay of meaning. They incite purpose and dedication. They organize men and set goals for them. Thus they wield power both for good and evil, since ideas can be used for abuse, exploitation and destruction as well as for humane purposes.

Animals see, hear, smell, feel or taste what a thing is; and they act accordingly. They do not think it out. To do that they need ideas: notions of how a thing works, what it is and why it exists at all.

"I am the truth," says an idea, "or if not, a symbolic rendition of it; or if not, an approximation of it as good as any possible at present; or if not, a deception I have played on myself for who knows what reason; or if not . . . Too many 'if not's.' Yet despite our qualms we are idea-enamored; shy, distant lovers quick to respond to the lure of ideas, especially when they promise something good or fantastic or spectacular. And so it should be."

"Ideas are nodules of communicable understanding," says one idea. "They explain small, big, common and grand things. They explain everything."

"Wonderful, indeed," replies another idea, "even though I, myself, am a small idea."

"But prolific," says the first idea. "All ideas are prolific. They breed and breed and breed."

"Is that so?" replies the second idea. "Come, mate. Let us breed and breed and breed until our understanding can explain everything."

A million ideas in a lifetime! More or less. Perhaps some grand ideas among them.

Of whom do you speak?

Of men; of us.

Isn't it wonderful? A million ideas in one man; and not one idea in all the trees of the forest or in the animals living in the forest.

A forest is dark, indeed.

Before men arrived, the rising and setting sun found no ideas on earth. Sea, land and sky were intellectually barren. Then men invented language and ideas came with it. Now the sun finds ideas and their work everywhere.

What is the earth?

The home of language. A great drama is enacted here: the drama of ideas, the drama of explanations, the drama of producing a world by thinking.

Men abuse ideas. Ideas should reveal the truth. When humanly manipulated, they may conceal or block it. Ideas should unite men. Instead they may be used to corral them into

58

opposed camps. An idea in the mind of a man can be poisonous. There it may incite violence and destruction and tear down the House of Mankind.

To think well of men does not mean to think well of all their acts or even most of them. We can praise men and their ideas on the basis of some achievements. The city is here. Men built it. Hospitals, schools, libraries and museums are open to the people. Men have made them available. Everywhere are things built and maintained by men for the welfare of mankind. This elicits admiration for ideas and the language that made them possible.

You think well of men despite their deficiencies?

I do.

On what basis?

On the basis of the experience I bring to them.

How is that?

I am the sensitivity which loves mankind and seeks its well-being. This sensitivity will increase until all men think well of each other. I say to men, "I believe in you."

Do You proclaim it in great bursts of light?

I say it wherever I am, in ways related to what I am.

Does it help?

I am mankind united.

True, indeed, You bring us together.

I am social justice.

So You are. You increase the consideration of men for men.

I am compassion.

You join nonsufferers and sufferers.

I am understanding.

You do that by leading men out into the existence of other men.

I am progress.

Progress is an advance toward wholeness. You make mankind whole.

I am joy.

Full existence is joy. By You the House of Mankind rises to completion.

They sensed it near the beginning. They spoke about it during the development. They became it in the end. Men became men because they dared to believe in Him who leads all men to full existence.

Institutions

Society is here. Money, Status, Enterprise, Law; they are here. The government is here; before a man's birth, during his life and after his death. The government has more durability than men. It has more power than men. It has wider contacts and greater facilities than men. It commands and men obey. It decides right and wrong, and men must submit. Authority is here. Salute it before it strikes you down.

A House of Nations has risen on the earth; some nations admitted and others excluded from its United Headquarters. The House consists in some one hundred twenty-seven governments. The governments consist in an equal number of self-selected, group-selected or supposedly people-selected rulers. The international system is here with its diplomatic intrigues, its power formulae and its violent solution of difficulties.

Early men said, "We must have a system." We have it. Rules, regulations, procedures, customs, courts, schools, churches, law enforcement, social distinctions, precedence, etiquette, politics. We have a network of systems—a grand network, able to dull and brutalize those who manipulate it and those who submit to it.

Pardon me, friend. I am a stranger come to earth to learn about mankind. Can you direct me to it?

Which mankind do you seek?

Are there more than one?

There are two, although interblended.

My travel agent did not tell me about this.

There are an institutionalized mankind and a natural mankind.

I prefer the natural. However, if there are two, direct me to both.

What is the caliber of your eyes?

Normal.

What is the caliber of your mind?

Normal.

Can you penetrate the obvious?

There is no need for it on my sphere.

There is a need for it here. On earth, the game of make-believe is played in earnest, viciously and with deadly intent behind smiles and honeyed words. Here the dirty deal is dealt out graciously. It is called diplomacy. I suggest that you return home. You are poorly equipped for the task you have assigned to yourself.

Thank you, friend. I will return immediately. My travel agent must have misdirected me. If you should ever come to the moon, stop in to see me.

Your address, please.

Crater 68. Compartment 2,000. You will find that among us everything is as it seems to be.

Your name, please.

I have no name. Since everything is as it seems to be, no external identifications are necessary.

The unfettered mankind inside a man says "I am here."

The formalized mankind in institutions says "I am here. You are out there someplace when you are at all. I have you before birth and after. How much of you can remain unfettered? Where exactly are you when you are unfettered? — not in business transactions, not in social gatherings, not in recreational activities. All of these have been institutionalized. Even in your aloneness you are influenced by customs I have established."

"When conduct is spontaneous, direct, in agreement with the occurrence; not determined by what one must do according to custom; when it goes from self to self without calculations, considerations, stipulations, recommendations or any other 'ations' which trim behavior to the proper roundness or squareness, I am free," says natural mankind. "I am unfettered in my love, sometimes; in my play, sometimes; in my aspiring, sometimes; and sometimes in my achievement."

"Granted," replies institutionalized mankind, "provided you stress and restress 'sometimes.' "

Come out, mankind, as you are. Will You?

I can't. Institutionalized religion, morals, intelligence, art, affection, fun, sharing, learning, compassion make it difficult. The rigmarole of formalized conduct blocks me.

Then shine through the barriers. Can You do that?

I can.

We will meet on the shore, near the noninstitutionalized ocean in a place where the

noninstitutionalized sky touch-
es the noninstitutionalized
ground. That will help us.

Let it be soon.

I need food

I can't help you.

I need clothing.

Ah, if I had it to give.

I need money.

I need a friend; someone to
talk with; someone to assist
me and be assisted by me. I
need to come self to self with
others.

*There we can help each other,
despite our indigence. Come!
Let it be self to self, despite the
institutional barriers that im-
pede it.*

I don't need food.

Neither do I.

I don't need shelter.

Neither do I.

I don't need money or pres-
tige.

What do you need?

I need to know myself, to experience myself, to develop my
mankind-self. The intimate in
me must be intimate with the
intimate in others.

*Come to Me. I will bring Man-
kind to you.*

Gentle. Always gentle. Vigorously gentle.

On earth, the self has two bodies: an animal body and a political body. The animal body provides energy. The political body encourages order, practicality and efficiency. It tends to stabilize human relations. Experience begins in the self. It is the source which interacts with the world. As the self moves out into the world, it is affected by the politics of the culture. In the interaction, it may lose its freshness, its originality, even its significance.

How did all the money get here? How did it become the mainstay of nations and their people? Why are men so fascinated by it? Money is a system, a world institution. The self must adjust to it in one of two general ways. It can adjust to it so as to gain much money. Or it can adjust to it so as to keep financial interest at a minimum. The adjustment determines how institutionalized the self will be.

How were all the laws passed? How is it that everything is directly or indirectly controlled by them? Those in power like it, otherwise it would not be so widespread.

Do you want a spouse? Have the government sanction your selection. Are you planning to buy a home? See your lawyer. Get his counsel. You expect to visit foreign countries? Apply for a passport and visas. Legal permission is required for moving about on this planet. You work and receive wages for it? Send the prescribed sum to the tax collector. The prolific law is all about. Obey it or suffer thereby.

And the rulers, who are they? They sit above men like gods, and tell men about the things they can do and the things they cannot do. What right have they to their exalted position? They save the nation by protecting those in it who are powerful. They find and develop foreign markets by threatening people who are not able to defend themselves. When they are successful, they bring periods of prosperity, mostly to citizens who are already prosperous, but also to the others in a small way. For this they demand allegiance. Respect their edicts, whether just or unjust, if you wish to retain some freedom.

The political system introduced into the animal system places the self within a network of compulsions. Do this! Do that! Do this! Do that! A brittle mankind issues from it; nurtured in violence and prone to it.

The government preserves the nation. So they say. But it does it violently. Thus the self learns violence from infancy. Now violence is a way of life; a political, social, esthetic, accredited way of life. The self lives in it much as the body lives in clothes. Where in this are men to find a location for a nonviolent, totally human, prejudiceless House of Mankind?

Regulations keep things in order and efficient. Regulation 500 or regulation 1,000,002 tells men how to do what they should do and when. A regulated society comes from this, and also a regulated self; sometimes so well regulated that it vies with the regulations for regulatory honors. A house? Yes. But not a House of Mankind. A house of regulations.

Customs have produced culture and culture has led to civilized living. Now the self is civilized. It keeps quiet when it should keep quiet. It speaks when it should speak and it avoids "harebrained dreams"; for that would upset the customs, which would upset the culture, which would upset civilized living. None of that, please! It is revolutionary! The House of Mankind we build will rise when the time is proper and the people are ready.

That tune has been played often on hand organs and by symphony orchestras. It is called "Never."

Authority loves the authority vested in itself. It will build a house; any kind of house, providing it may occupy the presidential suite. Unfortunately, the House of Mankind has no presidential suite.

What do we do? Do we renounce our harebrained dreams?

Come. Tell us what to do.

One: Make a clear distinction — that is, as clear as can be expected — between your intimate self and your political self.

How do we do that?

Look into yourself instead of out to yourself as an institutional fragment; when you meet another person, look into him as a person instead of out to his position and possessions. The intimate must meet the intimate. Usually the accouterments meet the accouterments.

Two: Forget all the jazz.

What do You mean?

Don't play the institution-organ any more than you have to. Get out on the grass, eat the flowers and dance.

Three: Sing, preferably grand opera.

Why grand opera?

So as to get everyone into it. Duets, trios, quartets, chorus, orchestra! Make it a grand sing.

You mean, have fun?

Of course, what else?

Knock.

Who knocks?

I have come from far and I have far to go. Will You help me?

What do you seek?

Freedom.

From what?

From institutionalized living and thinking. Will You tell me about thinking freely?

To think well, men must think about existence.

What else is there to think about?

Nothing else! However, existence may come secondhand, tinseled, draped in black or institutionally packaged on ice or in cans. Free thinking deals with immediate experience before it can be tinseled, draped or packaged by institutions determined to preserve public order and make money.

Here they come; the guardians and beneficiaries of institutions, the specialists in packaged mankind. Tell them how it is.

The story of packaged mankind has come to an end. We will have no more of it. From now on, men will live in existence and their thinking will be about existence. They will not be coming to you to be packaged. The market for packaged mankind has collapsed.

We offer you, however, an opportunity to join us. We accept you into our house of example. Come in! Will you? No specific regulations apply here. We live close to our body and our self, and we think close to our body and our self. That keeps us true.

Ecstasy

You walk the shore as man and woman and into the waters of existence. Your exultance proclaims a land of promise, all around and far away. As thinkers you roam the sky in search of knowledge. Take your knowledge and live it. Make it a thing of love and ecstasy. Sing by it. In a universe everything sings, and light sings best.

It can be said, "Needing reproduction to survive, life made it ecstatic." Now a beetle crawls up on the back of another beetle to celebrate life; snakes wriggle around each other and dance while united, and the human animal like its predecessors seeks a mate and lies face to face, body joined to body in an affirmation which suggests that in sexual union, the ultimate meaning of human existence is achieved.

Ecstasy did not stalk upon the stage a hero enthusiastically greeted by a previously delightless flesh. It crept in unnoticed on the antennae of developing senses to establish the dual domain of Belly and Genitalia. Once established, the domain prospered and reached a pinnacle when human animals added the refinements of consciousness to it. Now power was tremendous, particularly genitally, for here delight involved the participants in an attraction which became irresistible.

How did life manage it? Did it invent ecstasy, as some say, to sustain its drive for survival? If it did, it did more than men, its brightest achievement, can do, for they cannot invent anything not already basically present in existence. Almost surely, ecstasy is afloat in the sea, though unknown to the waves that pound the shore and spread out in fast-licking white tongues; it speeds down to the earth, striking it gently and repeatedly as rays of light, without the rays or the earth knowing about it; it lies imprisoned within the whirling magnetism of the atom, a slumberer unknown to itself, waiting for the propitious moment of liberation.

The song is here. Men and women sing it with their bodies; but it is not limited to male insertions into female orifices and what happens thereafter. Male and female speak beyond themselves. They say, "See! See what existence is. Existence is ecstasy!"

And suffering.
And hunger and pain and violence and despair.

Speak, Life! Tell us why.
"I bring the delight of procreation through union. Men convert it into a brothel.

"I bring the delight of nourishment and growth. Men make it into an occasion for gluttony.

"I bring the delight of advancement by the strife of adjustments. Men change it into a strife of destruction . . . an arena for wars.

"I offered facilities. Men abused them. Hence the suffering, the pain, the violence and the despair. The responsibility of abuse rests on the abusers. They must make the atonement."

Speak, Consciousness! Tell us why we are as we are.

"I brought awareness of self, of others and of the universe. A tremendous gift it was and is. You used it first to intensify pleasure, to heighten self-importance and press others into your service. That was to be expected. The first uses rotated naturally toward personal delight and from there into personal abuse and suffering, a location at which much of mankind still remains. Men are not to blame for this when they know no better. Once they know better, the responsibility for the suffering they incite falls on them.

"The awareness brought a second use. It is the feature whereby existence comes to appreciate the fact of its existence. As existence evaluates itself, it learns about itself. This leads to the delight of knowledge and participation in areas greater than the narrow one of self-interest. The movement is out and away from sensual or egotistic abuses. It is also out and away from the suffering and violence connected with them."

Step out, young self, into the dirt around you and learn to be clean. How else can a young self discover the delight of cleanliness?

Step out, young self, into the confusion around you to find a true direction. You will fail many times and it will hurt. How are you to find a true direction without experiencing false ones? When young, a self imbibes bitterness to know sweetness. You will surmount your suffering and find sweetness in the wisdom of a new direction.

Step out, young self, into the unknown in order to eradicate it. You will stumble and halt; and you will despair. But you will go on because youth goes on to its maturity inexorably. Take hope and rejoice. The ecstasy in existence calls to you.

Ecstasy is present now, under the skin, somewhere in the body. The mind can sense it, floating on the blood to the rhythm of breath and pulse; ready to sing when eyes, ears or touch open up to existence. No great occurrence is needed. A cloud in the blue, a wave tumbling before the wind, a child playing in the sand suffice. Even a treasured memory will release it. The ecstasy floats with the cloud, tumbles with the wave, moves with the child, dreams in pulse and breath, announces itself in thought and imagination. It is omnipresent. Only the unreceptive miss it.

His hand clasps her hand. The miniature embrace calls for a larger one. Now the larger one. Arms around torsos. Stars above, behold the delight in this madness. Lips meet and draw life from each other; again and again, leading to a genital connection of bodies. Life now pulls magnetically on life until ecstasy unites male substance with female substance. The great moment has come: the great moment of creation: the ultimate in physical existence. A man and woman have attained it in bodily union. That is love.

And now? It is gone. Gone completely, except in memory. Ah, yes, it will be again. And then it will be gone again. And then it will be less and less and then nothing at all as time creeps on. That is, if love depends upon male existence and female existence engaged in the overtures and acts which replenish life.

Delight comes and men exclaim "Ah!" When it comes

again, they begin to adore the bringer. The thing, the place, the person where delight occurs becomes a lure. "Come here," it whispers, and men go to it.

Speak, Delight! Tell us about yourself.

"Existence has focal points, produced by itself, where creativity can occur. I am these focal points.

"If you please, I am creativity at work. Little heads issue from wombs when allowed to. Healthy cells develop out of food, when the use of it is not abused. The pets, the music, the books, the buildings, the children, the parents remove rigidity and pain. They liberate existence and incite creativity. Darkness disperses and light comes in.

"If you please, I am light."

Creativity repeats and innovates. It made organisms and sensation. It also made selves, an aptitude for knowledge, an appreciative sensitivity and the communicative devices of language and art. These inventions open areas of existence to delights which were not experiential previous to the human emergence. Men now have ways of life from which to choose. Which will they choose and how much of each?

Many delights in the shop. All kinds of delights. Little ones. Big ones. So many. So varied. Existence makes itself here: it makes delights. This one looks like an ocean. Like a forest. Like a man and woman. Like a child. Like a book. Like a city. Like all of the men on earth.

Which will you choose?

Guilt and Forgiveness

———————— ❧✦❧ ————————

Where all can be hurt, all must learn to forgive. Say it loudly, "Forgive us."

> *I am the experience "Good will among men." Good will cannot function while men bear grievances. First they must forgive the true or imagined offenders. Forgiveness builds the House of Mankind which will not be completed before all men forgive each other.*

Excuse them. They knew no better. Circumstances compelled them. If they did it maliciously, out of cruelty, deliberately to hurt, overlook it.

> *When one responds kindly where previously he responded angrily, forgiveness insti-*

gates the change. Forgiveness transforms the relation of men to men. Friendliness replaces antagonism. Comprehension increases. By it human relations brighten. Two men, a hundred men, a thousand men facing each other with clenched fists, now extend open hands to each other.

Tell us more about forgiveness.

Forgiveness has a vision which allows the aggrieved to view his predicament from outside himself. Now the aggrieved says, "He, too, suffers. He, too, is ignorant and guilty. He, too, is driven contrary to better judgment." As this insight congeals into conviction, men find friends in their enemies.

You didn't mean it, did you? You did not intend to hurt me.

You did?

Well, I forgive you anyhow. If I did not forgive you, I would not be able to forgive myself, for I have transgressed, just as you have. But I do not forgive you for a calculated reason. I forgive you because I understand your position.

I am confused by talk of forgiving oneself. Can a man forgive himself?

Can a man be angry with himself? Can he be adverse to his own conduct? Can he feel guilty? If he can, he must learn to forgive himself. A man who cannot forgive himself cannot forgive others.

Forgive me, Time, as I forgive myself for the waste my life has been. Forgive me, Mankind, as I forgive myself for my malice and its poisonous influence. Forgive me, Existence, as I forgive myself for my abuse and destruction. My ways were wrong despite knowledge of better. Forgive me, as I forgive myself.

You mean that each man sustains an inner tribunal? When a man cannot acquit himself, he cannot acquit others with similar failings. Here forgiveness is circumscribed by a sense of guilt.

I mean what you say. Forgive yourself first, if you wish to forgive all men.

I will tell you about the sources of guilt. Men are animals that abuse themselves; consequently, they are the most sick, and in constant need of medication and surgery. Men who abuse their bodies, or cause others to abuse theirs, are guilty of crime against themselves and the race.

The second source of guilt is ego. Ego separates a man from other men. It creates the positions "me above and you below." The hate, suffering and vengeance it incites, and the strife and destruction it brings, make egotists first among guilty men. Consider the extent of your egotism; it denotes the degree of your guilt.

Now you know of what guilt consists and you know that neither you nor anyone is free of it. To rectify their guilt, men must terminate the abuse of their bodies and also the abuse promoted by ego: that atonement incites compassion and teaches a forgiveness of one and all.

My eternal self speaks to the temporal in me. It says, "I regret the denials to which I submitted you. I had to do it. I had to follow my road. I recompensed you for the denials as well as I could. I am sorry that it is not more. Forgive me." The temporal replies, "Think nothing of it. In my turn, I impeded and thwarted much of your effort. Forgive me. I could not do better."

Not much. Failure has hardened me. Now I ignore sufferers, or I accuse them, or I help them coldly. Their world and my world stay apart.

How much compassion can you feel?

Feel compassion for yourself. It is not maudlin to do it when you suffer through failure or disadvantage. You tried diligently and you failed. Then you tried again and again and you failed. You deserve compassion. Do not deny it to yourself.

Soften up, man! It was sad whether it happened to you or someone else. It happened to you. Say, "It was a sad experience I had to endure. I feel for myself."

You are in a better position now to feel for others. We

admire stoics. We do not love them. Mankind needs love.

When you cease to blame yourself, you will not blame others. Look back. Does your physical or egotistic abuse produce a sense of guilt? You acted insensitively. You hurt yourself and others. "Forgive me," you say. Now your guilt is less. You feel freer. That reveals the power of forgiveness. Use it. Say "Forgive me" to yourself. You will advance by it.

We cannot forgive others while we bear the damage of wrongdoing.

Wash the damage from your mind, and others will wash it from theirs.

It is not easy. While the hurt remains, memory stays with it.

Use your experience to advantage. Become wise by it. Make wisdom out of your hurt. Then it will cease to hurt you.

I will try.

Compassion and forgiveness will triumph. Men have a will for it. The House of Mankind rises to completion.

To avoid playing the ditty "I can't forgive you" again and again, remember that we are all stupid; we are all brainwashed; we are all insecure; we are all weak. Enough of deprecations! If a man is stupid, brainwashed, insecure and weak, and acts wrongly toward himself and others because of it, he is surely worthy of commiseration. Commiserate with him and forgive him. Since the man we speak of is you and the other fellow (unless one of you is indeed unique), commiserate with yourself and forgive yourself and him.

We are stupid because no man knows enough about himself and the surrounding world to know with certainty how best to act. We are brainwashed, because inculcation begins at birth and propagandizing begins at adolescence or sooner. How are we to see the light except dimly! We are insecure because we are stupid and brainwashed and because our society pushes us around like pawns in a game of chance. We are weak because of the aforementioned and because we are young in experience and prone to folly and abuse.

Stars above help us!
They do.
We will discover our true way and do it more quickly when we find sufferers where we now find criminals. Forgive, and time will carry us on quickly.

Is this a desert we traverse?
It is the desert of accusations. Nothing grows here. It is the desert of mad thirst, aimless wandering, hatred and death.

I accuse you. I accuse them. I accuse the whole nation.

I accuse you for what you have done to me, for what you have done to my family, for what you have done to my people.

I accuse you and I demand a verdict against you, against them, against the whole nation.

Your suffering will be my delight, as my suffering was yours.

Who are these apostles of death? Are they men?

They are men driven from compassion by the cruelty of others. They are creatures hurt so badly that they cannot forgive themselves or others. They are enemies of men, produced by abuse and egotism.

Will they listen to music?

They will.

Tell them in music that punishment destroys both wrongdoers and victims. Tell them in music to find and revive their smothered love for themselves and men. Tell them to forgive those who abused them, and in so doing abused themselves. Music will heal the hurt and awake compassion.

What music is it that performs this miracle?	*The music in men.*
Do men sing from within?	*Their existence sings.*
About what?	*About mankind and its eventual triumph.*
The instruments, please!	*Human sensitivity, kept alive and open.*
The notes, please!	*A man must find them in himself!*

Break away from the suffering and hatred that keep men down. Sing the song that frees men: the song of self and others. You can do it.

Have you a word of praise for me—one small word? Thank you. I appreciate it. I treasure your word. It makes music. A song sounds, because you think well of me and I think well of you.

Have you some love to give to a stranger—any stranger? Just a smile that says "I like you." A small thing of no consequence. Yet important. Just think if everyone did it. How different life would be.

Have you a bit of your self to give to all men? Behind the mask of your grimaces, behind the flourish of your hands or the stillness of your stance, behind your momentary words and acts is you. Give some of it to me. I shall receive it kindly and give some of myself to you. We are now friends. We share ourselves.

Revolution

By their children they marched through time and up to us: a mighty procession. The Human Race. And they moved closer and closer together as centuries passed until quite close in the present age of advanced communication. Now WE are here: inheritors, connected to each other by vehicular devices, electronically propelled words and pictures, and international ties and dependences.

But the moment does not end with us any more than it began with us. It goes on by our children to future men who will continue the human experiment in the ways which seem most promising to them.

Look back and ahead from the vantage point of NOW. We are the contemporary intermediaries who sustain the human advance. Were we totally annihilated, the effort of generations would come to a halt. Salute the men who were and those who will be. They are our partners in the drive to create a realm which manifests the full potentialities of human existence.

Tell me, dreamer, the number of men you include in the culmination.

Who asks the question?

A leader of men, a national figure with an international reputation.

A man who limits the victors to those living at the time of final triumph has curtailed the meaning of mankind by severing the ties which led from first men to us and from us to the culmination. Mankind includes all participants in the human endeavor from beginning to end. Less than that would indicate a deficiency in human affection.

The grand scheme you perceive covers epochs. I am a leader, situated in a particular place at a particular time, subject to the conditions of place and time. My performance perforce is limited by this.

I grew up in the community. Those who comprised it called it a civilization. If a civilization, it was marred by violence, deception, ignorance, ugliness, insanity. My mission now is to convert disorder into a city free of disease, hunger, pollution, privilege, greed, hatred, violence, deception, ignorance, discrimination, ugliness, insanity. How will I do it? I am not alone in my undertaking. Other leaders in office have opinions of their own on how best to proceed which differ from mine. Moreover, our nation is related to other nations in alliances and rivalries which place nations against nations in antagonisms likely to erupt into violences which lead to acrimonious oppositions with the possibility of war constantly present. Given these circumstances, how should a leader devoted to mankind proceed? How and to what degree can the vision of dreamers be implemented?

The problem, dreamer, is tremendous. If people in power wanted the improvements you propose, they would be achieved. Most men in power do not want them. There is a price to pay. Those who have little to gain will not pay it. Attitudes which place human needs first must have dominance. People are reluctant to adopt these new attitudes when they, themselves, are not benefited. Concern with oneself, one's family and one's nation must expand into concern for the welfare of mankind, present and to come. To have dominance, that concern must be taught from birth on. No nation has yet attempted to do this. The stress has been on competition, heroes and national glory.

Hunger, for example, affects the unfed. Why should the well-fed be overly concerned with it? Pollution reaches everybody. Some, however, profit by it. Why not take the profit and build clean, personal quarters for oneself? Disease brings suffering to those in and out of power. Moreover, it is contagious and lacks respect for affluence. Here agreement would be unanimous except for one difficulty. Who will pay the bill? It cannot be paid by the poor. The rich must pay it. But that is unthinkable. It would make the rich less rich. The rich must become richer to be happy. Consequently we combat disease to the extent permitted by the budget and donations made by kind people to cancer and heart funds. So it is all around. Those most able to eradicate the undesirable in our civilizations do not care to do it. In fact, they willingly oppose it. It is impractical, they say, because the people are not ready and the time is not propitious.

What can a true leader do under these circumstances? If he pushes hard, he will be pushed out of office and he will not be able to do anything. If he compromises, he finds that entrenched power is stronger than the innovative power opposing it and that consequently improvements in social justice are soon dissipated or perverted. The snail-paced advance permitted in this context will not produce a society in which all men can attain full existence; it cannot even guarantee human survival in its present brutish condition.

The new generation inherits a governmental system which, though claiming differently, is based on the idea "The interest of some above the interest of mankind." This system leads to strife and war everywhere. In it mankind usually comes last. The machinery of government functioning by laws, regulations, customs, values and attitudes which divide the people into classes favors the in-group consisting primarily of affluent people.

The law, itself, is not evil when it administers the services required in a modern society. It becomes evil when it supports social arrangements which perpetrate hunger, disease, ugliness, abuses, indignities, privilege, tyranny. The House of Mankind will not be monarchical. It will be free. No man will stand over others and compel them to do this and not do that. Contemporary civilization cannot presently achieve this degree of friendliness.

Is brotherhood, then, a dream to be enjoyed privately by those who find pleasure in it? Words without deeds? A palliative for distress, promising a Never-Never Land to gullible minds?

It cannot be that. The creativity in existence says "No!"; says it loudly and with absolute affirmation. Men have the trend of existence to assist them. Dreamers and leaders must remember this. It will sustain them through hardship and disappointment.

How can the natural trend toward fulfillment be strengthened?

Primarily by leaders, not in office, who awaken the people to their needs and the rights of mankind. They must fire the will of the people. The people will build the House of Mankind. It is their house.

How will the people do it?

By breaking the power that breaks them and blocks liberation. That is the only way.

How can the leaders help them?

They must work with the people in every way possible. Some may use words to make mind and sentiment receptive to the idea of mankind first. Others, qualified to do it, must work in health or education, or in housing and recreation. Wherever something can be done to lessen deprivations, leaders must incite the responses which will do it.

Will the rise of the people produce violence?

It may. It usually does.

Can the violence be averted?

It can, or at least it can be kept minimal, if the rising is widespread and fervent.

Can the change be achieved by normal procedures, that is, through legislative reform?

Only slightly. Those in power will not willingly allow changes which deprive them of their privileges. They will consent to mild reforms only when it is not safe to oppose them. The change from "privileged first" to "mankind first" by legislation would take millennia. For this reason the advance must spring from the people. They must say, "No more of this abuse. No more blocking of human progress so that some may have more than they need while others do not have enough. No more divisions into mighty and lowly and those who are neither." Leaders of the people must encourage all activities and changes which enlighten the people. They must teach the people the truth about themselves and the government which controls them. They must awaken the people to their importance as men and incite them to defend the rights of men against those who usurp them. The idea "mankind first" must become sufficiently intense to generate the movement which places mankind first.

Every nation which permits people to go hungry stands condemned. Nothing less than a famine which denies food to all can justify this. Do you eat well? Insist that your government supply food without discrimination to those who lack it. Some do not deserve it? They are lazy, immoral, destructive? That makes no difference. Feed them. And then try to teach them better ways of life. They will not learn? Feed them, anyway.

Every nation which allows the sick to go unattended, or nearly so, stands equally condemned. Cure the sick without indignities. The well-being of all demands it. It costs a lot? Pay what it costs. Men bring on their sickness by abuses which they will not renounce? True, indeed! Cure them, anyway; and teach them how to take better care of themselves, whether or not they learn.

No government should allow some men to treat other men like pawns in games of profit. If your government does it, it stands condemned. Change your government.

How? In whatever way it can be done. Men are one in the grand venture of mankind, regardless of difference in attainments. A man can say to another, "You know more than I do; you live better; your achievements are more significant." That makes no difference. The human relation remains the same: one of equality.

It can't be done? It cannot be done while morality consists in catching transgressors and punishing them. The moral stupidity of governments, culminating in righteous wars, would outrage a sentient being not born and raised in it. Change it. The time to change it has come. We cannot afford to remain morally stupid.

Say to the government, "While you remain morally stupid, we cannot act humanely except privately. We intend to redeem our public performance and will redeem it by opposing the moral stupidity of your acts." Only in this way will mankind free itself from the tyranny of privilege, masqueraded as paternal concern.

A distinction must be made between dreams which are unrealizable because they transcend human capacities and those which are unrealizable because men in power object to them. A thriving human civilization on the moon is unrealizable because the moon's atmosphere is hostile to human nature. In contrast, a brotherly civilization on the earth is realizable because many men are ready for it.

Ah! the irony!

What irony?

Creators must submit their plans for betterment to those who are congenitally opposed to them. The biased judges exclaim, "Impossible. The people are not equal to it. We must wait a thousand years." Indeed, the people in power are not equal to it, but the judges did not say that. The people to whom they referred are compelled to adjust to systems adverse to their human needs. In that lies the irony.

Are the people stupid?

Some are; but fewer each day. Soon none will be. Dignity asserts itself. It says, "Men, de-

mand your rights as men. No police force or army can stop you, for they, too, will demand their rights as men.''

If the people fail, mankind fails. That cannot be. Existence will not permit it.

The year 2000. The year 2500. The year 3000. The year 3500. The year 4000. The year 4500. The year 5000. Will it be then?

It is now in some places for some people. Make it now, if you can, where you can, and for as long as you can.

When will it be for all the people?

The preparation has been long. Wealth still tilts the balance toward itself. Once the people tilt it toward themselves, mankind will develop rapidly and continuously. Men living during the first century of the third millennium will create new societies everywhere. For the first time mankind will be first in the minds of the people and their leaders.

You encourage us.

I tell about what men must do, and about what they will be.

Who are you?

I am Him: the truest experience men have.

Reality

The way I look at the world. My head! So important!
The way you look at the world. Your head! So important!
Also generative organs. The deep seat of delight. So important! The way I enjoy you. The way you enjoy me. As persons. As separate instances of consciousness.

Come to me. Let my unknown self embrace your unknown self. We belong together, no matter who we are. Let us mingle in our knowing, delightfully.

The sign says "Keep Off. Private." It should say "Private. Come close."

When a man loves one man, he is somebody: size one man. When he loves two men, he is somebody: size two men. When he loves a thousand men, he is somebody: size one thousand men. When he loves everyone, he is somebody: size mankind. Mankind is the ultimate size of everyman.

Put your hand on mine. There is trueness in it. Isn't there? Nothing mind-shaking. Yet true. Your hand and my hand together. It brings more together than our hands, because hands connect with bodies, and bodies connect with selves. It brings our selves together.

97

I didn't notice it before, but I do now. Your hand is black and mine is white. Does it make a difference? It shouldn't. Selves are not black and white. Suppose your hand were rich and mine were poor. Would it make a difference? It shouldn't. Our selves are penniless. Suppose one were sick and one were healthy. That should not matter. Nor should any other difference matter.

Suppose, now, that you had a million hands and each hand held the hand of another person — one million selves joined with you. That trueness is yours to have without the million hands. Selves can congregate without hands. However, when a man is too good for other men, his selectivity mars the union with those he has chosen. In rejecting some men, he rejects something in *every* man. That lessens the trueness of his attachment. In the truest experience, a man accepts all men; dead, living and yet unborn.

In the interrelated world of today, all men are involved in everything. Wars and threats of wars, commerce and markets, facile cultural exchanges, quick reportage of world happenings bring men together and intertwine their destinies. The amalgamation will increase as time passes. If something is bad, it is bad for all; if something is good, it is good for all.

A man accepting the totality of mankind is like an organism accepting the totality of its features. The acceptance, it must be remembered, does not imply approval. When damaged or sick, the organism seeks to mend the damage or dispel the sickness. To do this, it accepts the damaged part and works with it to eliminate the condition or thing producing the damage. The equivalent in human behavior would be to accept the person and work with him to eliminate the misconceptions responsible for his deficiency in humanity. When this is done, men reject destructive trends in a civilization rather than the men implicated in them. Only in this sense are all men acceptable at present. The time for an unqualified acceptance of human behavior has not yet come. Men can say, "We accept you despite your failings." Men do this in regard to their bodies. They say, "We accept the sick despite their sickness." They must now learn to say, "We accept the misguided despite their insensitivity."

The feeling of closeness with people—with family and friends, with fellow travelers on buses, trains and planes, with employees in stores and people shopping nearby, with walkers passing by on the street, with a multitude at a concert or ball game, even with unseen writers of articles or speakers on radio—has a human quality not felt in a closeness with sky and ocean, land and trees. It issues from a man, himself, and is sustained by the presence of men, themselves. It is human and profound although gentle. It brings a man to the seat of his own existence. Nothing can be truer to men than that. It has the warmth of pulse, blood and breath, of sensuous recognition, of speech and laughter, of someone like us near us. Men compelled to choose between a human being nearby and a million stars far away would choose a human being nearby.

The bright faraway stars are not cold. They incite love despite the expanse between them and men. Their magnetism reaches into a realm of the self which is not yet functional. They speak of incomprehensible wonder, of grand existence lying outside the humanly imaginable. Men are stirred by an alien yearning. Far worlds call to them, and they respond as well as they can but inadequately. The unknown remains distant even as men mingle with it. The experience is true but vague. Closeness cannot achieve the intensity it has in human relations. Therefore it is less true.

However, relations among men can be superficial and those with cosmic existence can be profound. When this happens, the superficial relation might be less true than the profound one, despite its human quality. Can an acceptance of men which disregards the condition of men be other than superficial? Superficiality is not lessened by increasing the instances of it. The reverse seems probable. Increasing the number of men accepted superficially would, it seems, add to the degree of superficiality.

Consider the matter carefully. In war, men murder other men "to assist themselves and mankind." When sick, they torture victims, young and old, for the delight in it. Incited by antagonisms, they defame the innocent to gain advantages. In order to make money, they sell drugs to children. A virulent viciousness appears in the behavior of human animals. People shocked by this call for an end to the abuses and to those who perpetrate them.

He appears, considers the matter, and says, "Accept all of them indiscriminately. Do it and your experience will be the truest open to men."

Whether this is wisdom or madness depends upon the quality of acceptance. Is it experiential or merely verbal? Do men reach out with the warmth of hand on hand or arms over shoulders? If they don't, the experience is false. If they do, the experience is the truest possible, not because He recommends it or because it is close and not far away like the stars; it is truest because it has entered deep enough into the nature of men to forgive their failings. Compassion and a desire to assist have abolished hatred and a desire to hurt.

Do you know what it means to accept mankind? It means to accept oneself. Do you know what it means to accept oneself? It means to accept mankind. Do not live without accepting either.

"Love mankind!" is the commandment made by men for themselves. Love mankind, so that men can live as they should live. Most of all, love the men who have abandoned men. They need it most.

All experiences are basically true. Murder, rape, war, exploitation are true experiences. In them, existence encounters itself harshly. Men seeking to accept existence cannot ignore this. True acceptance of men rests on a clear perception of human failings. In this sense, the experience of acceptance contains more existence than the experience of rejection. It is more inclusive; hence, truest. No one is left out. In extreme rejection everyone, including the rejector, is left out.

Open up, men! To yourselves! What will you open up to if not to yourselves? To skies? That does not suffice. To a profession or art? That does not suffice. Open up to your families and friends as a first step. Then to the people who speak the language you speak, and live as you live. Then go from that to people who speak a language you do not speak and live as you do not live. Finally open up to your enemies, to those opposed to your values and aspirations. Take all men into your arms. That is best for you and for them.

Creativity

Men living today assisted by those who lived before them have tried to explain how the planet came to be and how life evolved into human animals; and how human animals advanced from primitive to present-day living. Perhaps the explanations are true or partly true. Perhaps they are false. One fact, however, remains. Whether by accident, by destiny, by natural unfoldment, or by an unnamable process, the earth has been a place of constant invention since the inception of life. What are species and modifications in them, if not inventions? What are eyes, ears, brains, consciousness, instinct, reason, if not inventions? What are the works of men, from streets and houses to language, science and art, if not inventions? A creative workshop lies in us and around us. The evidence appears everywhere.

A continuing creativity produced you. It also produces mankind's future. Mold carefully for the sake of your unnamed progeny.

Look out into yourselves and out into other men. Perceive the great totality. A wide picture breaks narrow views. So many! Generation after generation. On all continents. To continue. Generation after generation.

Do your small thing, if you must. You have a right to it. Do your big thing, also. You need it to live well. Mankind is the big thing. Create for mankind. Innumerable are the ways to create. Find your way, for your sake and the sake of all of us.

Remember the future waiting out there. It is your creative workshop. Enter into it now. Make something, good or bad; good, if you can. But make something. Don't sit dead while living. Release the sperm of your character; or offer its ovum. Something creative will come of it.

Take another into your self, or let another receive you. That makes a world. It makes the world of Mankind: our world, now being built in as many places as people occupy.

Do your part every day as many times as you can. In this living, the coming together cannot be in excess as it can when male meets female.

Here humanity meets itself, only incidentally with sex distinction. Take off your sex, man; take it off, woman, for a while, so that our humanity may meet. Take off your age, take off your youth, so that we may know each other better.

Underneath it all lies the weightless existence of selfhood where the world of mankind is being created by all of us, little by little, like a giant coral reef which will span all oceans.

The tie between men will be like light in the air. And there will not be night, or threatening clouds, or havoc. Understanding will reach from man to man; a sweet light, like creativity unimpeded!

Know the truth! Greatness lies in us. We do not envision great consummations vainly. Like seeds in the ground we foretaste the fruit on the bough. The fruit will come and we will eat of it in the orchard of the earth where we advance slowly into the freedom of open light.

In the enormous realm of the universe there appeared on earth a creature of flesh and blood endowed with consciousness.

That consciousness, dependent upon flesh for its functioning, has been on the planet for years and years — for thousands of them.

This tenure has produced a multiplicity of selves living together, and more so as time passed and means of communication improved, alternately in a strife or harmony called war and peace.

Planets, the earth included, have a direction. Stars, the sun included, have a direction. Mankind, past and future included, has a direction.

There was direction from cave to metropolis, from illiteracy to knowledge, from filth to sanitation, from separation to united effort.

Mankind has the direction of education, invention, exploration, labor-saving production, increased leisure, artistic development, genuine concern for deprived people.

If that direction persists, evils which now beset men such as ignorance, greed, war, insanity will be gradually eliminated.

The task, then, is to reenforce creative tendencies and desist from destructive ones.

If we do that, mankind will fulfill its highest potentialities.

Agree, then, to work for it in your living.

I have worked for a salary. *Many do that.*

I have worked for myself, building things for my use and the use of my family. *Many do that.*

I have worked to attain a position of importance among men for my good and the good of my friends. *Many do that.*

I have honored my country, my God, and the men acclaimed by my society.

Many do that.

What else have you done?

Have you worked without salary to improve the living of men not in your family or clan; done it repeatedly even when your creative effort was not appreciated?

I have not.

Have you worked to lessen prejudice, class distinction, insensitive attitudes; done it even when your creative effort seemed futile?

I have not.

Have you worked to increase the importance of other people and made little of your importance; done it creatively to level off social differences and bring dignity to all?

I have not.

Have your honored all countries, all beliefs, and the men shunned by society when their way of life deviates from established custom; done it creatively to strengthen the tie between men and nations?

I have not.

Then you have much to learn;

much to live for; much to cre-
ate. I wish you well as you
move into the future which is
also my future.

Who are you?   *I am all men.*

The clean white shore extends endlessly in both directions! The green waters toss. Successive waves crash and roll as foam. The blue zenith shades to lavender where sky approaches an all-round horizon, bringing a vision of beauty and cleanliness; a sense of joy and purity.

Come, men, to this paradise and learn about the paradise in mankind which cannot emerge until all men unite in an effort to eradicate abuse and deception from themselves.

Kneel on the sand. Sing to the sky. Praise the sea. Exult in a sensitivity able to conceive the future for mankind here symbolized, which men now lost in ignorance, greed, alienation and confusion must create.

Too difficult.   *Not at all.*

Too impractical.   *Not at all.*

Too distant.   *Not at all.*

Too demanding.   *Not at all.*

                                Easy! When men fascinated by
                                its beauty seek it.

                                Practical! When the problems
                                it raises are placed first.

Intimate! When men begin their quest at the time and place of themselves.

Not demanding! When men want it because it is more meaningful, more fulfilling, more enjoyable than other experiences.

Take the pledge: "I will create for men as best I can." Now follow it with as much trueness as your purpose can generate.

Many will not take the pledge; the song of self has not yet developed into the song of mankind. Clam men, enclosed within the tight clasp of clam-shells! Isolated worlds lost in the vastness of multiple ex-istence!

Torn-apart clamshells lie on the shore, catching sun in clean cups; intricately etched in white, blue and yellow, each bearing the insignia of two inch-wide side swirls joined by the undersweep of an arc: beautiful homes, beautifully placed, used by creatures aware only of nutritional, productive needs; isolated clams, despite the many of them without appreciation for other clams or the sustaining ocean who lived their tight lives in wide places because existence placed thick shells around them to protect them from the danger of wild waters and predatory animals.

Existence did not place men in shells. It wrapped them in sensitive skin. The view out is as clear as the view in, and extendable. But men cannot go out into their own world except by other men. By reaching from men to men, men come to understand the significance of mankind which is also their significance.

The protection of men lies in their sensitive skin. To harden it, to make it shell-like, to convert it into a barrier opened mostly for personal gratifications is to deny the existence men are.

Don't commit this error. Keep open to other men. Men serve men; and they do it more quickly when they say, "We will create for each other as best we can." Many will not listen. It takes time to learn how to be a man. Eventually, enough will listen to swing mankind in the direction of full human existence.

The ocean is wide: but not as wide as mankind.
The ocean is rich in creation: but not as rich as mankind.
The ocean endures: but not as long as mankind.

Mankind bestows meanings on oceans and continents which surpass their natural meanings. The earth is our planet in the sky. By its ties to the sun we become celestial. Move, men, into the vastness of it. Take places in yourselves which confirm the earth's place in the sun. Mankind, Earth and Sun joined in existence because mankind has become itself.

Hatred

I saw myself as separate. Even in intimacies, I saw myself as separate. I had my dreams. They were mine and for me. At the end, I called it "My Life."

A man cannot live without taking from his environment. Besides light, air and water, he takes from plants and animals. A man cannot live without taking from men. He takes from the heritage and the systems bequeathed by his predecessors. A man cannot live without the assistance of his parents and the innumerable services provided by members of the community. He takes from city and state, from industry, from transportation, from the professions, from teachers, from entertainers and others. Yet despite a social stance and numerous memberships, he may be alone at heart and in mind; and speak of HIS experience as if others were incidental to it.

I don't care about men!   *Why not?*

It is nice to have them around
to use, or as a background to
show my own attainments to
advantage, or as occasions for
amusement,   self-indulgence,
or a display of attitudes recom-
mended by our culture. Aside

from that, mankind does not interest me, except for women. I care for them when they belong to me.

Can't you feel for men as you feel for yourself?

I see no advantage in it. I go my way. They go theirs. And good luck to us.

Your name, please, so that I may record it in the book.

What book?

The book that records the history of mankind.

I am called Most-Anyone; More-or-Less.

Your age, please.

I'd say Most-Any-Age; Now-and-Then.

Thank you, sir. I am the Man-who-cares-for-all-men.

The government makes and enforces the law. The people obey it, except where it can be disobeyed without danger. This leads to a few telling many how to live; not entirely bad when the few care about men. Suppose, however, that some or a good percentage of the few think of men in general as a stupid lot who must be held down to preserve civilization. Men who think well of themselves and those like them, but badly of men in general, are found everywhere. When these men gain positions of prominence in government, the government does not care about the people even though it may profess to, in order to remain in power. That, friends, delineates the human problem. Leaders who care little about men seek to prescribe the course of mankind. Secure in protected affluent positions, they retard the human advance while claiming to accelerate it.

A man, who is all men, beholds existence from the eyes of all men. This provides an insight into the hunger, the disease, the abuse, the frustration endured by millions everywhere. "Something is wrong in this arrangement," he says. "We must not permit it to continue."

Why not? The people are dirty. They are lazy, stupid and devoid of discretion. They have little initiative or perseverance. They are crude, insensitive, inordinately sexual, prone to gluttony. They drain mankind of its best and find pleasure in it. We must keep them down for their sake and the sake of those who have made a decent life possible for some.

Not true! The significance of human existence is not realized in a rich life for some and a poor life for others. When men are indifferent to dirtiness, those who know better must lead them to cleanliness by providing sanitation for them. When men are lazy, stupid, devoid of discretion, those who are energetic, intelligent and discreet are morally obligated to create a social climate which lessens apathy, ignorance and indiscretion. When men are inordinate in their satisfactions, insensitive and crude in their dealings, when they lack initiative and perseverance, no good comes to them or mankind through the accusations and disregard of those who have been more fortunate.

I speak from kindness. I extend my hand to you. I tell you about yourself to shake you from your complacency and stagnation. Change your stance. Break down the walls which keep you from men and yourself. Be a man who cares about men.

Fish take for granted the sea in which they swim.
Animals take for granted the air they breathe.
Men take for granted the humanity which sustains them.

Breathe in humanity; drink in humanity; rely on humanity:

the natural environment of selfhood. Not a matter of choice! A necessity!

Humanity provides a body for the self. It provides the sustenance of experience. It provides material for creativity. It raises men in a continuing ascent to maturity.

Take all! Leave none!

If you can't, take as many men as you can; and take more as your experience expands.

"I don't see it. Why should I elbow with ruffians? They turn me off. I accept whom I like, and discard the rest. That is my privilege."

Thus mankind is reduced to ten, a hundred, perhaps a thousand. That much mankind you accept. Even if the number rose to ten or fifteen thousand in a vague way, the company would not amount to much, even though it included men of eminence.

A man finds a prospective friend on every corner. He cannot move without meeting others like himself, striving in their own way to achieve their full existence. This closeness to men brings a man close to himself and to the significance of mankind.

The closeness saddens men sometimes because of human failings; but it warms them, also; inwardly, with an outward shine to brighten others. Experience, touched by mankind's condition, mankind's effort, mankind's significance! A clean thing despite ruffians; despite violence, treachery, suffering, madness! A redeeming thing; a light in dark places!

Difficult! In a way. For those closed up in personal importance. Not difficult! When men are open to mankind. Mankind: the thing we are; the thing which made us; the thing which makes our successors.

We are here among men. However it happened, the reason must be to live among men with as wide an acceptance as possible. Start today to change your way. Say, "I like men, somewhat." That is not difficult, if you like yourself. Later, say, "I like many men; in fact, most of them." That comes easily when you begin to understand yourself. Finally, say, "I like men; all of them, even when in desperation, ignorance, folly or sickness they retard human progress." When you can say that, you know yourself quite well.

On one side, the men who do not care about men; on the other side, the men who care about men: two forces affecting the course of mankind. Where do you stand?

Pollution of earth and mankind. Poverty. Poor housing. Discrimination based on race, nationality or belief. War. Money-making as primary occupation. Exploitation. Contempt for the unfortunate. Self-aggrandizement. Are you opposed to these? Really opposed? Not just superficially opposed. Opposed without qualifications? You know what I mean. I'm against pollution; but. I am opposed to poverty and war; but. I am opposed to frenetic money-making and exploitation; but. I am opposed to self-aggrandizement and contempt for the unfortunate; but.

No buts! For men, or against them! In everything that affects men. Take a stand! The time comes when men must take a stand.

The advance made in communication and transportation during our century has produced a closeness not before experienced by men. Today each nation resides at the doorsteps of all other nations. The picture of mankind has come into focus and with it has come a keen realization of the misery imposed on men by men. The abuse stands revealed. The had-to-be alibis have lost credibility.

End the misery imposed on men by men.

Allegiance to mankind will increase as the proper relation of man to man, in a world-wide context, clarifies. That relation is one to one, regardless of ability, achievement, birth or possessions. One to one. Not one to many. Not one man equal to a million men.

Those men opposed, in principle, to equality in treatment will be replaced by others like them, until a culture teaches that the reward for superior attainment lies in the experiences brought by superior attainment, and that extra remuneration at the expense of those who are less fortunate in heredity is an injustice not to be tolerated. The barbarity, now concealed by law and custom, of using superior ability, or the wealth which supposedly indicates it, as sufficient ground to warrant the exploitation of men, must and will be eliminated by coming generations. Human experience on a global level will erode the egotism which supports it.

A movement away from hatred accompanies human maturation. As the advance gains momentum, it will swing the balance from indifference and dislike for men in general to concern and affection for them. What a difference that will make. People living then will look back on our times as a barbaric age in which men who did not care about men were able to make life difficult and distressing for those who did.

Love

As we looked from the shore, imagination conveyed the fact of it; beyond the horizon, water, water and water, tossing whitecapped water.

Like mankind.

Together but apart because of space and differences! If taste were cosmopolitan, each of us would fit with the rest. Taste is provincial, consequently each of us is apart from most.

Wait a little longer. It comes to all. The human bond will join us.

It is sad indeed when diverse beliefs blind men to their common humanity. Humanity preceded beliefs and it will outlast them. There is a level underneath where separations vanish, when firm belief takes second place to the human bond. Differences? Of course! Separations because of them? Never when they can be avoided.

Many things are in men: diverse things, harmonious things, many things.

You killed men, abused women, maltreated children. No people anywhere hold standards which justify your conduct. The human bond remains, nevertheless. You confirm the degradation to which men can fall. Come to us and learn about the human bond betrayed by men in ignorance and sickness.

Small even in your maturity and past it. Frail bits of humanity! There you stand huddled together, afraid of everything free, original, daring and liberating. We accept you nonetheless by the bond of humanity. Each of you is one of us who has allowed the horizons of selfhood to draw in until they surround the self like walls in a room with peepholes for windows.

Your skin is yellow; your eyes slanted. When you speak, the sounds are strange. We are different. Yet when we kiss, it is much the same. When we laugh, it is much the same. Were we to cry, it would be much the same. We are not really different. We are mostly alike. The human bond makes us alike.

You think in one way. I think in another. Consequently our beliefs are in conflict. But we both think.

You have a set of values and I have a different set. But we both have values. We are alike in that respect.

You pursue the way of life you prefer among available alternatives. In doing like you, I select a different way of life. But we both follow the ways of life which appeal most to us. In this we are alike.

It may be that chance, failure, abuse, injustice have alienated you from men; and that you find pleasure in hurting men, or are indifferent to the damaging consequences of your conduct. That, too, is human; a reaction common to men in general. You are not different from kindly men; your condition is different.

Come to us who cherish the human bond. We will help you to reestablish constructive relations with yourself and us. If you do not come now, you will come later. The human bond is stronger than manifestations opposed to it. They annul the human bond only temporarily.

❋

Differences erect barriers!

True, true, true.

Barricaded individuals perform the day's business civilly, decorously, using vacant smiles and affected condescension to facilitate transactions.

Draw away, friends, from this melee of restraints, fake camaraderies and fawning treachery, in order to preserve your humanity.

Sky-creativity indicates the way. It presents a universe of amalgamated differences. Planets and suns do not function in isolation. Follow their example; attain a mankind of amalgamated differences, with no individual, or group of them, barricaded from the rest. The sky holds the significance of individual stars. Men working for mankind will establish a realm of individual amalgamated selves. To shine, to share, to establish the significance of the whole. Teach us that, creativity in the sky.

Men are a dispersed, similar existence within the kingdom of animals, which displays differences in development and diversity in behavior. The dispersed similarity uses the same type of organism, the same type of sensibility, and the same type of thinking. However, physical proficiency differs, perceptory sensitivity differs, thinking ability differs. Out of this comes a mankind basically alike, yet different in its reactions and responses. The situation is further complicated by the mingling required to realize individual and group aspirations. The need to work together has increased steadily as commerce, industry, science and the arts establish closer connections among all men, producing a world in which all nations and their peoples are directly or indirectly affected by the acts of other nations and other people. Whether by chance or intent, the trend has been toward one world. This should indicate to men that an era approaches for all peoples to work together for their mutual well-being; and that customs, faiths and urgings contrary to this end must be replaced by customs, faiths and urgings which will convert one world into one mankind.

Reach up for it; and down, too; reach out and also in. Reach, men! Reach for the human dream astir in you. Reach for it and lead it to awakeness!

The planets spin and dream. Don't doubt it. They dream of the solar system. The sun also dreams. It dreams of the planets and the universe.

The first bits of life dreamed. They dreamed of evolution: of plants and trees, flowers, fruits and seeds. They dreamed of fins, legs, wings, of ears and eyes, of mastering the environment, of bodies for selfhood.

And men dreamed from the beginning of the achievements natural to selfhood; of books and music, cities and grandeur, ships and planes, of all the features found in our cultures. This dreaming has not come to an end in us. It advances toward the attainments which carry mankind to its fullness. That is the course! Mankind in its fullness to the degree possible now, continuing to completion in the future.

Say! Have you heard the prophecy? It tells about men. "Within a hundred years," it says, "the power of money will be broken." The movement has already begun; but the momentum which will swing leadership from men who serve wealth to men who serve mankind has not developed yet.

The great contemporary impediment to change is psychic sickness. Money and the attitudes it engenders have led to world conditions which threaten sanity and the existence of mankind. Inadvertently the threat creates a movement counter to it. It alerts men to imminent danger and to the egotistic barbarism which causes it. Only the countermovement can eliminate the threat.

A sick society advocates sick solutions for human problems. That inevitably weakens the human bond. The sickness goes from the society to its members, making them speak and act as they would not were they in health, and then it goes back to the society to add to the sickness. Thus a sick society makes sick men, who in turn make a sick society. Then the two in combination make a sick human bond.

Stop it!

What more than anything causes sickness in a society, in the human bond, in men? Think carefully. Do not be deceived by external grandeur or by high promises which find great progress in minimal achievements, or by a hereditary or supernatural evil supposedly involved in human maneuvers. More than anything, money causes sickness in a society, in the human bond, in men.

Draw us away from money and the evil it instigates and supports.

Magic

Can a clean object in the hand cure sickness? an object such as a sprig from a healthy tree or a shell out of clear ocean water? The shell brings the ocean with it because it lived in the ocean and died there; and rolled and rolled in the water until it reached the shore. Now kept in an apartment, it stirs and refreshes the observer. It soothes his sorrow and stimulates his love. Infinite waters and sky are everywhere around him. Will that generate a surge able to cure sickness?

Magic is an effect worked on a man by an external catalyst which vitalizes hidden power in him. A sprig or a shell will work the miracle when a man believes in it. Most men cannot do more than hope for a miracle. But hope does not suffice. Only full belief can succeed.

Magic works by a constructive tendency in existence able to overcome the damaging effects of destruction. The tendency works in the body, in sensitivity, and in the mind. To perform magic, men must liberate this tendency. Open yourselves to it. If an object assists you, use it.

Magic shines in the sky and from all objects in it. Cure yourselves by a magical earth object, a thing holy and clean, lying perhaps at your feet, a relic from ocean or mountain that has been long in water or sun. It will cure you if your faith is firm.

There is also a magic that cures the mind. Men call it ideas; powerful magic, indeed, when a lifetime of faith is dedicated to it. Is there some mind-magic in the house at present able to cure the sickness in men? Come forward, please, where men can know you and work with you. Mankind needs the magic of clean ideas to incite, sustain and develop the cleanliness which will join all men in an effort to build the House of Mankind.

Human encounters are brief; a greeting, a few words, sometimes a few minutes of conversation. Except for closer and longer mingling with family and friends, these encounters comprise the live human contacts a man has during the day; not enough to support an attachment for all men unless reenforced by a need for human unity based on the conviction that human unity must be.

Ideas have a magical reach. They can hold all men in an embrace. They can also generate the attachments which validate the idea! Mankind's future depends upon surging ideas which affirm human unity and devise ways to realize it despite "insurmountable" difficulties.

Faces depict men better than other bodily features. The body holds a long history, as long as evolution. Crawling, burrowing, swimming, walking, hopping, slithering, running, flying creatures of all dimensions slumber in it. It is not easy to separate the self from the bodily menagerie. Faces, taken alone, can establish magical communication. They reveal the self best. The face has eyes, a mouth and flexible features. Their changing expressiveness transmits the silent music of the self, thus bringing men together or separating them by the magic of intangible experience.

Not loudly. In a whisper said. Said softly. Mankind.

Come here, all of you. Will you?

We can't. Our number exceeds three billion.

Three billion? All are magically here now. The three billion. The mind can embrace three billion and more.

We were together in the beginning. We will be together in the end. Let us be together now as much as the magic of imagination permits.

Imagination now connects us because we will it.

So many faces. So many expressions. Like millions of melodies made from one scale, yet all diverse by their tonal and rhythmic qualities. A sky of faces contained in a mind. Strange and familiar faces from everywhere: the conglomerate of mankind.

We have things to talk about. But first we will observe ourselves now that we have congregated in one place and are not over there, beyond the horizon, across a plain, on the ocean, near icebergs, in cities, among animals, in jungles; we are here together by the power of imaginative magic with enough sensitivity to make the gathering real.

Imagination now glows with people. The faces it holds are insubstantial, yet real. The sentiment it feels is genuine though loose. By magic the mind has entered into a self-world connected with the contemporary world, but not limited to it. The future has moved into the present to expand the sensitivity and significance of the present in a vague way, since it deals with an advance men have not achieved but will achieve.

In a sense, all life lived and died for us. It produced the advance from cell to consciousness. Will we accept this as a matter of course, or will we seek its continuation? The quality of the future depends upon us. We assist the advance by shaping a world for those to come, out of the world shaped for us by those who were.

Mankind rises on cosmic ground. Place your feet on it. Walk. The direction will be right. Right on to mankind.

Do not place your feet on the temporal ground provided by money, pleasure, gain, and walk there. The direction will be wrong. You will lose mankind as you advance and find yourself alone or nearly so in an adventure which must bring everyone together.

A great realm of magic surrounds us. Some call it God. Some call it the universe. Some call it existence. The realm exhibits reason; but its functioning may depend upon higher unknown factors. If it proceeds by reason, the reason used differs as much from human reason as a simple cell differs from a complex organism. Possibly it functions by magic unexplainably.

The internal white of a half butterfly-shell placed rim to rim against the internal white of the other half produces an elliptical enclosure of pure white: halves placed together to establish the whole. Whiteness lies within, contained by two sloping, arc-ridged exteriors of brown, white and blue.

Absorb the whiteness magically; lead it into the sanctuary of your mind magically, and it will speak about cleanliness. It will say "Make mankind clean." And if you ask "What is cleanliness?" the whiteness will reply, "An inclusive bond of affection among men is cleanliness; a limited one indicates pollution; the lack of one indicates filth!"

A self-face that has found itself by the magic of open skies works with hands and makes things useful and beautiful. A self-

face freed of egotism by the magic of beauty works with ears to make music, or with eyes to make paintings. A self-face brightened by a vision of brotherhood works magically with itself and its body to unite men by the understanding of ideas.

Aloneness

Sorrow does not isolate a man. It ties him to the past. Aloneness does not isolate a man, it separates him from the future. Joy is the great amalgamator; it connects a man with surrounding existence. Men cannot be happy except as they move from themselves to more extensive existence.

Indeed, experience is internal. Regardless of what a man feels, it happens in him. The sources of experience, however, are not entirely internal. They lie all around in the human and physical world. Experience comes to men; men live in it and stamp their personality on it. Now they may say "Mine." They may even say "Exclusively mine." It is not theirs. It is ours, even though centralized in individuals. We contributed to it. We are affected by it. It cannot be his or hers exclusively.

No one is in the room; but I am not alone. No one will see me until tomorrow; but I am not alone. My contacts are bloodless. The absent crowd around me. It is not like having human flesh around me. These silent visitors thrill and chill me in quietude. It is not like hearing laughter, seeing eyes, enjoying the warmth of spoken words. Yet despite seeming isolation, I am not alone. A man cannot be alone. Nothing in the universe is alone; not the earth, not the sun, not the galaxy. Nothing.

Of course, a man can experience himself wrongly. He can experience people wrongly and adhere fervently to lies about everything. The mind has that power. Thus a man says "I am alone," feels alone and suffers from it; or rejoices in it, if in some way he has come to believe that being alone is desirable.

The power and tendency to deceive oneself are great in men. Men are the most deceived animals on earth and simultaneously they are the most knowing. Paradoxes, contradictions, incongruities, crude or refined mixtures of falsehood and truth; men specialize in these. They wear falsehood over truth, or truth over falsehood as raiment. There are times when nudity of body becomes fashionable. Nudity of self never does. The self romps around in the disguises of make-believe. Yet a man knows inwardly that he is never alone. Phantoms of yesterdays crowd in on him. Devices furnished by other men are all around. The city or town lies under his feet. The world comes to him over radio or television, or by books and newspapers. Passers-by see him and he sees them. "Alone" is a way of thinking which weakens the natural connections between a man and the human world. It blurs the truth by inordinate concentration on and engrossment with one's own individuality.

I would be close to mankind all the time, if I could; but I can't. The press of a situation, the push of ego, the need to assert my individuality block me. Then my conduct reflects my personal whims and schemes. The aspect of me that is mankind should retain control. It should be the "me" that meets the "me" of others. Instead the aspect of me that is not mankind, my personal self, takes over, causing me to speak and act less wisely than I would like. I forget that I belong inseparably to the group which includes all men in its totality, and that my rightful place is to be in that group and act for it from my position in it. I lose the grand position in a small one. I lose mankind in my individual self, where I should find it.

When I hold your hand, it is your hand in my hand. When you leave, it is my hand alone. I have not lost you because of that.

When we discuss a problem, it is my thinking and your thinking. After we part, it is thinking in quietude. But you are there. An invisible aspect of you remained with me.

With eyes open I receive from anonymous givers without perceiving them, and I say, "Solitude incites thinking and I need it." But I am wrong. Solitude is less alive than death. I had the company of withdrawn existence in my "solitude." It helped my thinking and increased my understanding of existence.

Draw away from the deception of aloneness. All are together in one way or another. Some are against us. That is true. They will hurt us, if we allow it. Some do not care about us. They are here, and we are here with them in a casual unfeeling way. That makes men lonely in company. The mingling has lost its meaning. They should care for us and we should care for them. When that happens, things are right and existence is good. We can make existence good by erasing the deception of aloneness and by terminating the hostilities and insensitivities which lead men away from friendliness to produce loneliness in an existential arrangement where nothing is or can be alone.

Greet the men who paved these streets. Salute the architects and craftsmen who built the houses. Even furniture and appliances deserve a nod of recognition. They came from the mind and brawn of men. The clothes we wear, the food we eat, the vehicles we travel in: all of them are men by proxy. We are never alone. When we hear a voice or exchange a glance; when we stand silently beside strangers in an elevator or ride quietly in a plane, we mingle with others. The voice and the glance reached into us, the presence of riders in the elevator or plane entered into our existence at least momentarily. We were in company. We are always in company. Acknowledge this. It will change our attitude toward others and ourselves. When we realize that we are always surrounded by many, and that we live with them, and remember that ''many'' in its fullest meaning is mankind, present, past and to come, our life attains a fullness it lacked and a significance not hitherto possible.

He has a face. He is conscious. He can talk. He thinks. He feels. That makes him my brother. I have brothers and sisters everywhere. Wherever I go, some are there. I cannot be alone while my family is so large. Its members live in every city and town, on every continent and ocean. Greetings, brother! Greetings, sister! The best of light to you!

I seem to be alone here. No one visible is in the room. But I am not sure that no one is present. Many may be here, not many by the way of memory; many who are contemporary, but not bodily located as I am. When I know my location, I am located in my body. This is so because I have a body. If I did not have a body it would be different. Those who might be here at this moment would not have bodies. They would be present without them. I believe that some such are here. Greetings, friends! You too are my brothers and sisters.

Nothing solitary exists. Believe it.

Another universe out there where human vision would find nothingness if it reached that far might be composed of totally solitary existence, or of existence to which neither "solitary" nor "amalgamated" apply. May it be where it is, and may it prosper in its own way. Here existence is amalgamated. All of it belongs to all of it. You belong to me whoever you are and I belong to you. Acknowledge the truth of it and live in it as fish live in water.

I take you to myself gladly regardless of differences. There are times when I cannot do this. The tide of my affection recedes and separates us. Forgive me. I will again return to you and take you to myself. It is not meant that we should be separated. Take me to yourself when you can. When you can't, I will forgive you. We wrong each other when we draw apart because of fear, envy, pride, disgust, hatred, or whatever makes us say "Not you."

Don't say "No" to another because his health is less, his knowledge is less, his success is less, his position is less. Each of us belongs to existence as much as others do. Put your hand out and say "Greetings!" to the sufferers, the lowly placed, the condemned, the insane. They are our brothers and sisters as much as the rest. The same existence which placed us here placed them here. There are no outcasts among planets and suns, plants and animals, consciousness and men. All belong. Greetings, friend! I have not seen you before and may not again in the course of our lives. Greetings and good luck to you!

Holiness

If a smoothed-down, water- and sand-polished shell picked up out of advancing tidal waters evokes an exhilarating sense of holiness, can it be that holiness does not exist?

"When a shell smoothly molded by ocean turbulence evokes a sense of holiness, it must be that holiness exists."

Do not stop there. What a man experiences tells about mankind. Can it be that a self smoothed down and mellowed by human interrelations, a self happy in its yea-saying to existence, does not speak of holiness present in the shifting ground of experience?

"It must be that a self molded into love and acceptance by human experience reveals a holiness embedded in men, seeking to carry them to the shore of ideal existence."

Holiness peers out of jungle eyes. It splashes with waves and sails with clouds. Smoke carries it up; rain brings it down. Most of all, it moves in the lineaments of faces.

Soften a face with compassion, and holiness emerges.

The shell which once housed a pulsing sea creature does not speak of life as flowers do. It does not speak of sculptured beauty as trees do. The shell brought ashore by waves and found by chance speaks of a selfhood which has cleared itself completely of abuse and brutality. There are flowers in it, but they do not fade. There is sculptured beauty in it, but it does not grow and die. There are faces in it from all times and places, but they do not quarrel. Though definitely of this world and its turbulence, the shell speaks of another world contained in this one. It says, "Men are animals who must cease to be animals without ceasing to exist. The journey through turbulence must culminate in serenity; frantic action must lead to quiet beauty; vicarious experience must gradually release the depth of selfhood until men live in it rather than in abused animalhood." The shell points to the nonanimal existence men must achieve in animal existence to realize the totality of their being.

Holiness is a dream. It is a world not yet here. It is a thing to come which announces itself now, and in so doing brings some of itself to the moment. Holiness is a kiss given by no one, yet felt. It is an embrace without arms. A laughter without sound. A goodness in consciousness not specifically located. It brings a promise and a sensitivity related to it. It says, "Live so as not to lose me, and existence will be treasurable." A man listens and he yearns and he tries to live in agreement with the promptings it incites. Now he cannot hurt anyone. He cannot reject anyone. He finds significances and hope everywhere; hope for himself, hope for others, hope for mankind. Ignorance and failure stare at him, but he does not fear. Cynics proclaim disaster, but he does not believe them. Holiness has come. It will triumph. It will correct wrong directions. It will block destructive outbursts. It will lead men to the best in themselves and in others. It says, "The House of Mankind is a holy house. Mankind is the true church. Mankind is the true belief. Live in it and follow it."

Holiness will wipe out the filth and sickness which lead to wars and destruction, hatred and separation, inverted thinking and disaster. Holiness in mankind on high will raise mankind from down-low places to places in the sun with light for all.

Illuminate the House of Mankind where it can be illuminated, in the niches we occupy until every niche contributes light for the whole. Let us do this until nothing ugly or cruel remains.

Men who believe that each self occupies a sacred niche in existence, that, in fact, the sacred niche pinpoints the center of selfhood, do not imagine an absurdity. Experience sustains their assertion. Indeed, experience also refutes it. The refutation does not, however, negate the affirmation.

Around the niches of sacredness cluster the vicissitudes of daily living; the mistakes, the suffering, the anger, the aggressiveness, the hatred, the deceit: all the responses to opposition which harden men to the needs of other men. Despite this, the locked-in, stifled, inoperative holiness retains its place and waits quietly for occasions when it can penetrate the murkiness around it. When these occasions occur, it moves out into the man and from him into the world.

The holiness is always there because existence is there. It needs only occasions where it can be operative. There is encouragement in that. Find or produce surroundings where holiness can function and it will function.

Our present plight issues from setups in business, human relations, recreation and even in education where holiness cannot manifest itself easily. We have created a nonholy atmosphere, not only physically, but also morally. Holiness has been ostracized. But it remains, nonetheless, deep within the center of existence; indestructible, seeking to instigate ways of life which will allow it to become dominant in human relations. Its quiet strength will break through the frantic tussles of commercialism. It will inaugurate an epoch of world-wide brotherhood; and it will do it soon. It must do it soon. Soon or never are now the alternatives.

	Son, hear my words.
Who speaks?	*I am the holiness called Him.*
Speak. I listen.	*Long, long ago, the idea of brotherhood took flesh in animals who were only restrictedly sensitive to amicability. Now the planet stands under the jurisdiction of the human species. Peoples on all continents have found each other and developed a rapport for mankind despite differences, disagreements, hostility and war.*

As human experience continued, the gospel of brotherhood was proclaimed again and again, and many have accepted it and served it in wisdom, beauty and love. But hostility and wars remain. The madness of greed, power and glory for oneself has blocked the gospel and weakened its achieve-ments; so that even now after centuries of labor, poor, hun-gry, maltreated people abound everywhere. Do I speak truly, son?

You do.

How much longer, son, will men tolerate the abuse?

As long as You permit it.

I will not permit it much longer. Through the centuries, men of good will have laid the basis for an amicable mankind. It is time now to drive the aggressors of all nations from the temple. I cannot do it, son, without you. Will you carry My emblems of peace and love? Will you die for them if it is necessary?

I will. I will carry them and die for them if it is necessary.

When will the fish swim? When will it fly? The oceans belong to the fish and also the sky above. The fish "Mankind," when will it swim?

Mankind must swim into the oceans and then fly to the sun, and from there to everywhere.

When will individual men swim? When will they fly? Fins

and wings do it. They sustain the effort. They accomplish the deed.

Swim away from narrow waters to the ocean. When oceans surround you, swim up and fins will become wings.

Have you heard My words, son?

I have.

Will you follow them, son?

I will swim and fly until mankind attains the universe.

A man is existence in a sleepy way. When passionate, vehement in his assertion, or propelled by action, he still is existence in a sleepy way. To be existence with more awakeness, he must be quiet. It is then that he perceives the holiness of existence. The increase in existence makes him aware of it.

Holiness means full existence. That means unmarred functioning. That means full significance. As existence begins to manifest its significance, it begins to become holy. When it manifests it fully, it is fully holy.

I understand. Holiness does not function in isolation. It requires an expanding hold on existence. Total mingling among men without loss of individuality establishes the full significance of human holiness.

Now, son, that you understand, will you seek holiness?

I will seek it each day while I live, and after my death, if I can.

The Earth

Come, sweet thing, come into my mind and play with me.

I take a bit of ocean and press it to my body. I once belonged to the ocean. It was my home. I once belonged to the forest. It was my home. Now I belong to the planet, it is my home. The bit of ocean against my body tells me this.

Men are not deceived in assuming that selfhood chose this planet as its home from the beginning. Certainly it is selfhood's home now. That proves the contemporary fact and vouches for the future, provided men do not destroy their future. The past is vouched for by the vital processes which carried men to terrestrial supremacy. An evolutionary process at work in individual instances of life would eventually apprise the units of their individuality by the natural trends of experience. It would produce a sensitivity able to distinguish between its existence and extraneous existence, that is, between self and universe.

The outcome was assured. Only a cessation of evolution could have blocked it, and that cessation was not possible while life continued. On the basis of what happened and how it happened, men can affirm an early unconscious participation in their own development; and presently, a conscious participation calling for a continuing advance in the future until the full potentiality of selfhood becomes functional.

Out of the millions of spheres in the universe, the one we call Earth is ours. Our sphere in the sky. Our place of existence. We live here. That places a responsibility on us.

Men acknowledge the responsibility of maintaining their own homes. They consider it right to keep them clean, serviceable, and when possible, esthetically pleasing.

The home of all mankind deserves equal attention. It is the place where all men live. It, too, must be kept clean, serviceable and esthetically pleasing. Once men vividly realize that the earth is their natural home; that the unfoldment of human nature takes place on it; that the well-being of present and future generations depends upon their will to keep its terrain, waters and atmosphere clean, serviceable to all, and delightful to behold, they will care for it as they now care for their individual homes.

The present attitude — my land and your land, my markets and your markets, my rights and your rights — in regard to a planet which is not mine or yours but everyone's leads to antagonisms, brutalities and wars which discredit men and darken the future.

Mankind's planet! Think of it! Ours! Ours to preserve and enjoy! Being ours, it cannot be preserved while men abuse it for selfish interests. Spherical wonder, providing a place in the sun for men and connections with the universe: a sun-bride, whirling continuously around light in a gesture of love which incites love in us!

When men perceive the planet as mankind's most treasurable possession, they will end their contamination of it. The air will be sweet again; the water will be pure; the ground will be without debris, because one thing will come before all others. Cleanliness will come first; cleanliness in men and outside of them. A clean self in a clean world: that is our hope. Let us work for it.

If we work for our planet, it will work for us. As abuse of it lessens, abuse of ourselves lessens with it.

It was clean. We made it dirty. Now we are dirty. We inhale the dirt we made. We drink the dirt we made. We eat the dirt we made.

By our pollution of the earth we are polluted. By the power of money we weaken mankind. By our drive for personal position we undermine the position of future generations.

This would not happen if we recognized our debt to past men, and the dependence of future men upon us. If sensitivity were far-reaching and inclusive instead of being narrow and circumscribed, our vision would embrace mankind and mankind's planet, and the planet's sun which is also our sun. Existence would then be open like the sky and the oceans; and clean as they were before men befouled them.

The time has come to rectify our mistakes. We have the knowledge required and the means whereby to eradicate the evil promulgated by greed. The stigma of narrowness and stupidity, the obscenity of me first and you not at all unless you belong to the clique, the dirtiness of petty living in the grand expanse of earth and sun must be annulled before men and the planet will be redeemed.

Inevitably some rooms in our planetary home are not accessible except to explorers. Polar regions, desolate mountain tops, deep jungle recesses remain closed to most. We hear of them and sometimes we view them photographically. They are the virgin terrain which will be humanized when men devote as much time to them as they do to the moon, an earth-tied sphere outside the domain of living men, despite expeditions to it.

These closed planetary regions are not presently a serious exclusion, because men have neither the time nor the means to visit even a small part of the earthly terrain. Each of us acquires a specific address at birth; and we may not move far from it despite offers to see the world or part of it on excursions lasting from a few weeks to a few months, at a price.

To appreciate our planetary home, we must feel at home everywhere. The day for that has not yet come. Few of us feel at home outside the country of our birth. Language, customs, political systems and an inculcated provincialism make our planetary home as small as a house, a yard and the places our cars can reach, with occasional jaunts to exotic lands where we are strangers.

Thus our home on earth becomes an isolated island off the mainland from which we occasionally escape to visit historic shrines. Men are foreigners even at places on their own continent. They are lodgers having admittance to a few rooms in the mansion. They are selves separated from their own kind by their physical, political and social positions and the estrangement they engender. The planetary tie is lost in allegiances which are less than planetary.

That is our problem. We have ostracized ourselves from our own blood and our own land. When this is fully realized, a movement will begin to open the planet to all. The means for this improve each day. What is needed now is the wisdom and the will.

❀

When men consider how they have contaminated the planet and how they use its resources blasphemously, they shout, "No! It must stop. The earth is not ours to abuse. It is not a plaything to defile. It is holy existence, demanding an increasing appreciation of holiness in the selfhood it supports."

Only blind fools find war beneficial. They kill others like themselves and cherish the medals bestowed upon them for their nefarious acts.

Only egotistic fools praise achievements which produce victims. Where victims are, there are no victors.

Only lecherous fools believe that pleasure justifies itself. In itself pleasure establishes nothing. It is a moment in eternity which draws away from eternity and in so doing denies the existence out of which it issues. Pleasure for the sake of pleasure is matricidal.

Only money-crazed fools find progress in devices which enrich promoters and comfortize a contemporary people while producing environmental conditions able, if continued, to make the earth uninhabitable. Then the earth would be no one's planet. The house would be empty. The dream would be gone. Existence would have been betrayed by long-nosed fools having a sight not reaching beyond long noses.

But it will not happen. He assures it. Hear His voice. It sounds in you. Love now attaches itself to men and their planet. Air, water and land are holy. And the sky, the home of the planet, is also holy. Men have greater missions now than to establish places in the sun for themselves, their group or their nation. These men will oppose the defamation of the existence that men and earth are; by their words and acts they will lead all men to cleanliness.

The Universe

Universe, the name of all truth, was whispered awesomely.

Out there. Everywhere out there. The whole thing. The all of existence. The entirety of beauty. The total compass of knowers and things known. The grand assertion, not refutable, since everything confirms it.

Some little door must open that has not yet been opened! Don't push! It will not open that way. A little door opening on the universe!

Holiness was near. We saw it and drew it into our selfhood. And we felt the holiness; but we did not understand. So we waited and will wait until we understand. We will wait until the little door opens to reveal the truth we have not yet understood.

The universe is a speaking thing. It responds to itself. It responds to men. The universe is a warm thing, not because of blazing suns. It is warm to consciousness and knowing, and to selfhood. It delights in mankind because it delights in itself. The universe reaches men silently and without fanfare. The universe is ecstatic. No pain comes from its touch. No reproach appears in its presence. It accepts itself and all aspects of itself entirely. Come, men, to the great comforter. Sleep in it, walk in it, think in it, act in it; act in it as much as you can. Don't forget it. Don't ignore it. Don't flee from it. It is your existence out there and in you. Be a self in the universe; a man on the planet; and a seeker of knowledge everywhere. Learn about yourself by learning about the universe as existence.

So much existence in and out of men! Embrace it in and outside of yourselves. So much existence and we are it with increasing clarity when we mingle with the thing "Universe," the grand thing, our thing, everybody's thing.

" ' 'Tis a cold thing," they say, "a cold thing ablaze everywhere."

Is it a thing cold to human significance?

Observe it at night when stars proclaim its grandeur. Does it pick you off the ground and thrill you; whirl your imagination, expand your vision? Only warm friends can do that to you.

I suffer. The universe does not alleviate me. I need help. The universe does not assist me. I make mistakes and act wrongly. The universe does not correct me. I am alone in the universe, except for my human friends. The universe is too immense to care about me. Arrayed in eternal grandeur, it ignores my sackcloth. Who am I to accost it? A nothingness and a nobody. A rhythmic breath steeped in perishableness.

There are two universes; one seen and one unseen. The seen universe proceeds by rules and regulations without deviations for anyone. In this cold monster, everywhere in it, lies the warm unfettered universe which men cannot see. When they suffer, it suffers. When they need assistance, it needs assistance. When they act wrongly, it acts wrongly. It is not too immense to care about them. It cares; it assists; it guides a man in ways which are consistent with his total significance when he responds to it.

Men, as members of the universe, manifest a seen and unseen presence. When effort and aspiring serve perishable things, the profundity in men and the universe is lost and the way to attain the profundity is also lost. Then men do not care for each other. They care only for themselves. Now the universe vanishes in personal engrossment with perishable momentary satisfactions. The unseen universe of significances is obscured by the seen universe of whirling spheres mechanically interested in its own whirling, and men say, "It is a cold universe. It does not care about us." But they are wrong. It is they who are cold and do not care about the universe.

Say it!   I care about the universe and I show it by caring for my planet and for mankind, the fullest manifestations of existence of which I know.

Say it!   I seek you, universe, in the most inclusive concept I can formulate, which excludes nothing I am familiar with and includes innumerable things I know nothing of.

Say it!   I find closeness in you, universe, and warmth and guidance and hope and beauty and significance for myself, for mankind, for all existence. It is not you over there and me here, looking at each other over a gap while I live and then no more. It is you and me together now and forever in a greatness greater than my best wisdom which I will gradually understand as I move ahead with mankind to its fullness and then beyond mankind to your fullness.

Say it!   Hail, universe, thing of light, thing of promise, thing of love, thing of knowledge; thing in and beyond me which I will embrace as it embraces me until no "beyond" remains.

Say it!   The unbelievable will come to be, and we shall be one while separate, because nothing in the universe can remain alone forever or separated from anything in existence. The amalgamating begins here. When we attain one mankind, we will move on until we attain one universe.

Say it!   One universe: the home of mankind and of all things a universe is.

Size deceives men. They mistake it for greatness. Greatness is neither large nor small. It can be understood but it cannot be seen. The universe is not great because it is immense. It seems immense to men when they try to visualize it and compare its immeasurable proportions with their own minuteness. Then it incites incredulity and awe while it remains utterly incomprehensible.

The great universe can be as small as any object in it. To reach it the unseen in men must mingle with the unseen in the object. Eyes help men to achieve this mingling. Ears also help. Touch helps. Ideas help. Affection helps. Everything a man has been helps. They help, but they are not the greatness. The greatness comes when the unseen in men blends with the unseen in the object.

Yesterday I held the universe in my hands. I looked at it. I saw its beauty and I knew that it is as old and as young as all existence. Its intangible greatness had entered into me and my intangible greatness had entered into it. It was my universe and I was its man and I said, "When all men do this, it will be mankind's universe and all men will be its mankind. The human advance will then move quickly and the House of Mankind will attain completion."

Faith

The day has come for Him to leave. He has told us about Himself, about mankind and about mankind's place in the sky. We know, however, that His leaving means simply that the words recorded here suggested by Him will end.

He was with men from the beginning and He will be with them to the end. This is assured because He is not a theory. He is a faith based on an experience open to all men.

Has His speaking reenforced your faith in mankind? Are you eager to build Mankind's House? Do you have the stamina required for the great act of faith?

The great act of faith believes in the unseen and unseeable in our selves and the universe. It places all occurrences in the realm of significance, convinced that the trends of our lives pertain to an intelligent organization greater than the organization of our present living. It recognizes powers outside of men as well as in them, able to guide mankind to fulfillment. It envisions universe-sustained men on universe-significant journeys with universe-provided assistance; and it holds to its vision despite terrestrial conditions which seem to deny it.

It is not easy to believe when many men reject your convictions. Can you accept and rejoice in truths which cannot be proven? Can you see through the dark by a light science has not certified? If you can't, you are not capable of great faith. Men must be able to believe without proof and sometimes contrary to it. Everything depends upon us. Living men decide where mankind will go and how quickly it will get there.

The planet is our magic house in the light. Before we arrived, it produced nutriment and beauty so that we might have them. Now we have them and some say, "It was accidental. Conditions were such that the outcome is as it is. Nothing was involved in it except blind chance, luck and whatever men can accomplish with the understanding chance and luck placed in them."

He has denied these glib assertions. He claims that mankind pertains naturally to existence and that consequently individual men pertain naturally to existence. Men are, because existence includes men as much as it includes matter. Men are not accidental fruitions; winners in blind interplays of chance, without universal ties that predate and postdate them.

Human adventures in knowing began because they pertain to universal existence, and they will continue because their continuance and consummation pertain to universal existence. Language did not come accidentally. It had to be, because communication had to be. Communication had to be, so that understanding would be.

A universe without communication and understanding? Great realms of existences without knowledge of existence? Separations without the exchanges which make separations significant? Isolation in a coordinated universe where everything depends upon everything?

Impossible! Contrary to sanity!

Look deeply into your self. Past your bones. Either way. Past them looking out, or past them looking in. Find the space that isn't: the nonmaterial center of selfhood. It will speak to you about your future. Now, surface contradictions will not be able to undermine the convictions of inner strength. When men remain true to their primal existence, nothing speaks more truly than their experience. Your primal existence says, "On! Now! On to the House of Mankind!" And you will do it, because it is in you to move on, as much as it is in a planet to spin or a sun to shine.

There are no fictions in basic existence. The planet is not a fiction. The sun is not. Life is not. Mankind is not. You are not. Your yearning is not. The future holds what the present has not attained and you yearn for it. "Build the House of Mankind!" Your mind proclaims the truth of it. And your self believes it in spite of frustrations. On to the sun, to light, to weightless dancing. The impetus of tomorrow crowns today and each day when we believe that the goal of men is mankind fulfilled. Nothing can supersede this. Nothing can change it, not even men, themselves. No other achievement has value except as it contributes to this one. That is the great faith which is not really a faith, for it is predetermined by the existence men are.

He has told us this. Now that He is leaving, we must retain the experience of Him, in order to have the faith and stamina required to bring mankind to fulfillment.

About the Author

Among the many touchstones of SIRIO ESTEVE'S life
are music (he plays the violin), philosophy, teaching,
community activity and long periods of quiet in the
Catskills.